Spellbound
Festive Beading
Three

A Spellbound Bead Co Book
Copyright © Spellbound Bead Co Publishing 2017

First Published in the UK 2017

Printed in the UK by WM Print
for the Spellbound Bead Co

ISBN - 978-0-9565030-8-4

10 9 8 7 6 5 4 3 2 1

Editor: Jean Hall
Pattern Testing and Sample Production: Edna Kedge, Pat Ashford, Vicky Pritchard and Ellen Morgan
Photography: Spellbound Bead Co

Visit our website at www.spellboundbead.co.uk

Spellbound Bead Co
47 Tamworth Street
Lichfield
Staffordshire
WS13 6JW
England

Call 01543 417650 for direct sales
or your local wholesale distributor

Also available by this author:

Spellbound Festive Beading
ISBN 978-0-9565030-2-2

Spellbound Festive Beading Two
ISBN 978-0-9565030-5-3

Spellbound Beaded Tassels
ISBN 978-0-9565030-4-6

Spellbound Floral Jewellery
ISBN 978-0-9565030-7-7

Acknowledgements

Thank you to everyone who has contributed to this book - the scrupulous bead counters, passionate pattern testers, an oh-so-patient photographer, a computer-fixer without equal and several top-notch tea makers.

Also a big thank you to all of our customers who show boundless enthusiasm for beading and baubles.
This book is dedicated to them and to everyone who has a passion for beads, colour and all things that sparkle.

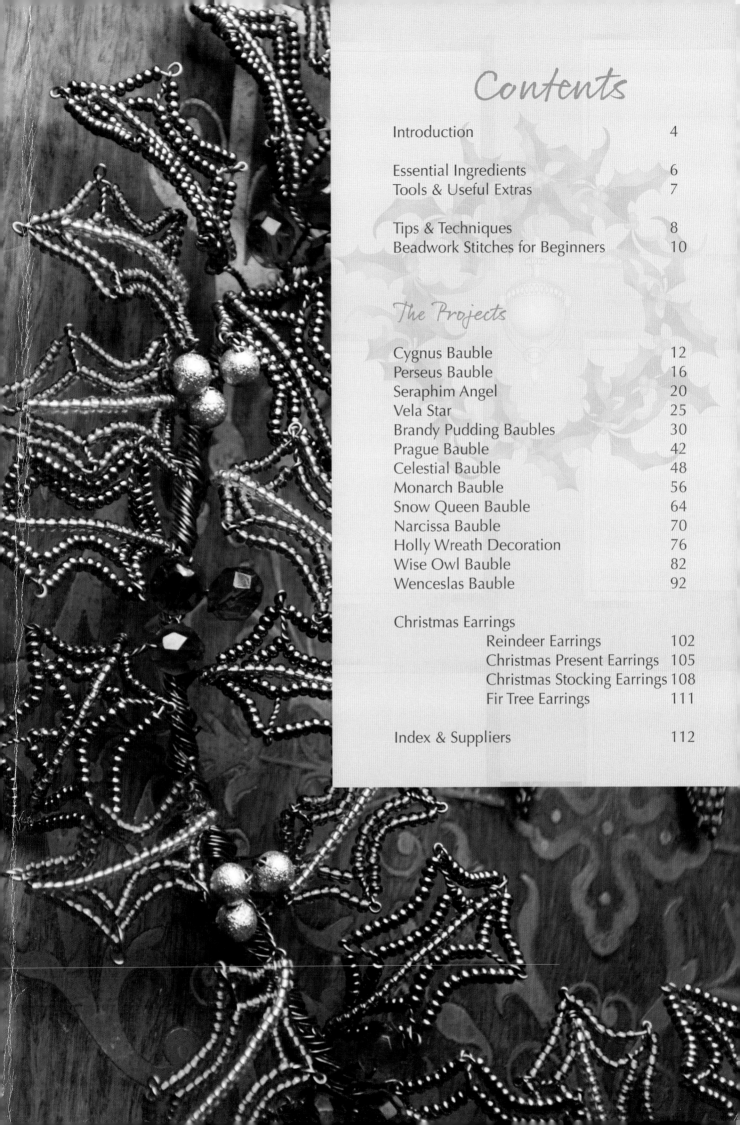

Contents

Festive Beading Three

Welcome to the new Festive Beading collection. This is the third book bringing together all things beady, baubly and beautiful to decorate your home.

The first two Festive books have become standard bookshelf requirements for beaders old and new, crafters and decorators. However we know they do not sit on anyone's bookshelf for long, as there is more to be found amongst the pages than just Christmas - motifs for jewellery, card-making and tassels, fringes that will adapt for furnishings and little novelties for that special gift.

To make this collection extra special, three projects - the Cygnus, Perseus and Narcissa Baubles have been designed by Pat Ashford. When we were small Pat taught us, with immense patience, to knit, to sew and to be creative. Thank you Mum.

The majority of the projects in this book use very basic equipment - just a needle and some beading thread. There is a fabulous wirework project but as the technique is deceptively simple, you'll just need standard wire cutters, round-nosed and flat-nosed pliers.

Innovations in glass technology and creative input from manufacturers have led to a profusion of multi-hole beads. Very similar to toy building block makers developing fancy-shape bricks, suddenly there are lots of new possibilities, although as beaders we now have double-holed tiles, triangles and faceted lozenges rather than axles and turret tops.
Several designs in this book utilise the more readily available of these double-hole beads but the other 'ingredients' will be familiar to all - seed beads, bugles and faceted glass.

Look out for the Extra Info boxes. They contain hints and tips on the techniques and materials you will be using in the projects.

Choose a Project to Suit Your Beading Experience

One Star - very easy - this project will be quick to make.

Two Stars - simple techniques - this project will take a little more time to complete.

Three Stars - getting a little more complex but manageable for a beginner with patience.

Four Stars - several stages building on top of one another. Each stage is straightforward, but there are more of them to follow, so it takes longer to get the finished result.

Beading can be the most relaxing and absorbing of pastimes; just you, your beads and the quiet concentration of counting... with of course, the bonus of making something beautiful, elegantly luxurious and intricately detailed.

Starting with the elegant and easy to make Cygnus Bauble, you will find something to suit every beading mood and beading ability.

The projects take you through one step at a time: from threading the needle to finishing the last thread end. Everything is graded for difficulty (see above) to help you to choose between a quick 'beading fix' and a longer more complex project.

There are Inspiration mini-projects within a couple of chapters for you to develop a motif a little further, but you will soon see many more possibilities. There are butterflies and stars galore; leaves and berries; bows and a tiny crown perfect for a clothes-peg king.

It's now just a matter of selecting the first design to make, an ooh and ahh over colours, perhaps changing your mind two or three times (we all do it) and getting started.

I hope you find it fun; you make some wonderful things; and you make time for the occasional 'gosh...I made that' moments.

Happy Beading !

Julie

February 2017

Essential Ingredients

The projects in this book all use a very simple selection of beads. For a lot of the designs you will need just two or three colours or sizes of seed beads, one size of bugle beads and a selection of fire polished faceted beads. This quick guide will give you an introduction to these basic supplies and the few extra items you might need for some of the patterns.

Fire Polished Faceted Glass

These hand-faceted beads are heated in a kiln to give the glass a glossy finish.

Used to add weight to fringe strands and sparkle to strands of seed beads, you will find 4mm, 6mm, 8mm and 12mm in most recipes plus faceted drops in the Monarch and Narcissa designs.

Bugle Beads

Bugles are small glass tubes which are available in several lengths. Most of these projects use size 3 bugle beads which are 6-7mm long, or a size 2 bugle which measures 4-5mm in length.

Colours & Finishes

Crystal - a transparent plain glass that can have further effects added to it such as a silver lining or an AB coating.
Silver Lined - a metallic silver deposit on the inside of the hole which glistens through the glass and makes the beads sparkle more vibrantly.
AB - Aurora Borealis is a thin rainbow effect applied on top of the glass bead for extra glitz.
Frost - an acid-etched matt finish applied to a glass bead.

Delica Beads ™

These tiny, cylinder-shaped glass beads are used for accurate weaving as they will sit close together like bricks in a wall. They are available in several sizes and hundreds of colours. This book uses only size 11/0 Delicas.

Twin Beads

Twin beads measure 2.5 x 5mm. They have two parallel holes which are suitable for a size 10 beading needle and size D beading thread. They are manufactured by Preciosa in the Czech Republic. Please also see Tips & Techniques.

Tile Beads

6mm square and approximately 3mm thick Tile Beads have two parallel holes. Be careful if using the AB version of this shape - the AB finish gives a different effect on each face so make sure they are all the same way round.

Seed Beads

These are the small glass beads used for weaving and stringing intricate patterns, tassels and fringes.

Seed beads are available in many sizes. These sizes are quoted on an inverse scale so size 6/0 is larger than a size 10/0.

These projects use size 6/0, size 8/0, size 10/0 and size 15/0 seed beads. If preferred you can substitute size 11/0 for size 10/0 seed beads in most of the designs.

Seed beads are manufactured in the Czech Republic or Japan. Czech seeds tend to be more rounded than the Japanese seeds so it is better not to mix the two types in the same project. All of the designs in the book are made with Czech seed beads.

Beading Thread

Sold under many brand names such as Nymo and Superlon, beading thread is available in several thicknesses and many colours. These projects all use a size D thread.

Wire & Findings

The Holly Wreath project uses three different diameters of coloured wire. A soft wire is required to prevent any brittleness and make manipulation much easier.

Filigree Bead Cups are used to make halos for the angels on the Celestial Bauble.

Fishhook Earwires are comfortable to wear but you can substitute post & ball or clip earfittings if you prefer.

Jump Rings are the connecting links used in all sorts of jewellery designs.

Tools & Useful Extras

Threading Necessities

Beading Needles

Beading needles have a very narrow eye so they can pass through beads that have a small hole.

Size 10 Beading is a general beading needle that is suitable for most of the projects.

Size 13 Beading is a little finer for multiple passes of the thread through the bead holes.

Sharp Scissors to trim the threads close to the work are essential.

A Thread Conditioner such as Thread Heaven helps to smooth the kinks in the thread if you get into a knot or tangle.

A Fleecy Beading Mat with a slight pile will stop the beads from rolling around and make it easy to pick up small beads using the point of the needle.

Clear Nail Varnish is sometimes used to stiffen selected areas of stitched beadwork so that the desired shape is firmly retained.

Pliers

You will need pliers for the Holly Wreath project and for the earrings chapter.

Round-Nosed Pliers for turning loops.

Cutters for trimming wire to length.

Chain-Nosed or Flat-Nosed Pliers for gripping, and opening and closing jump rings.

Tips & Techniques

There are a few basic techniques that you will need to know in order to work through the projects in this book. If you need a special technique for a particular project it will be explained within that chapter, but for the techniques that apply to most of the designs this is what you need to read.

Using a Keeper Bead

Before you start a piece of beadwork you will need to put a stopper at the end of the thread. The easiest stopper to use is a keeper bead.

A keeper bead is a spare bead, ideally of a different colour to the work, that is held on a temporary knot close to the end of the thread. Once the beading is completed the keeper bead is removed. That end of the thread is then knotted securely and finished neatly within the beadwork.

fig 1

To Add a Keeper Bead - Position the keeper bead 15cm from the end of the thread (unless instructed otherwise) and tie a simple overhand knot around the bead (fig 1). When you thread on the first beads of the pattern push them right up to the keeper bead - the tension in the thread will prevent the keeper bead from slipping.

When the work is complete, untie the knot and remove the keeper bead. Attach the needle to this end of the thread and secure as shown opposite.

Correcting a Mistake

If you make a mistake whilst you are following a pattern remove the needle and pull the thread back until you have undone the work sufficiently. Do not turn the needle and try to pass it back through the holes in the beads - the needle tip will certainly catch another thread inside the beads and make a filamentous knot that is almost impossible to undo successfully.

If you are working with a double thread, carefully pull on the thread to bring the blunt end of the needle backwards through the beading. Take your time and the needle will be guided back through the exact path it had taken previously and you will not cause a knot.

Making A Wire Loop With Pliers

Hold the cut end of the wire in a pair of round-nosed pliers. With your other hand, grip the wire 8mm below the plier jaws to give firm support. Roll the wrist holding the pliers to form the loop. Make sure it is properly closed and centralise the loop above the beads with the tips of the pliers.

A Note About Baubles

Baubles are made by many different manufacturers – some are hand-blown, paper-thin glass and others are machine-made in both glass and plastic.

Hand-blown baubles can vary a little in size from the stated diameter so you may need to adjust the bead count slightly if you are making a closely-fitted design. The variety of neck sizes across all diameters of baubles, both hand-made and machine-made, is quite marked.

Most of this designs in this book require a close-fitted ring of beads around the neck so you may need to adjust your bead count accordingly. Guidance is given where necessary if you need to make adjustments.

Starting a New Thread

On occasion you will need to add a new thread to the work.

Work the old thread until you have no less than 15cm of thread remaining. Remove the needle from this thread end and leave the end hanging loose.

Prepare the needle with a new thread and tie a keeper bead 5cm from the end.

fig 2

Starting about 15 beads back from the old thread end pass the needle through 3 or 4 beads towards the old thread end.

Make a double knot here (fig 2). Pass the needle through a further 4 or 5 beads and repeat the knot. Pass the needle through to emerge alongside the old thread end and continue the beading.

When you have worked on a little, trim away the tail of thread and the keeper bead as close as possible to the beads for a neat finish.

A note of caution - before you make the knots, make sure that the needle does not have to pass through these beads again. If it does, just leave the new thread end attached to the keeper bead without any knots around the existing thread. You can return to the keeper bead later, remove it and attach the needle to this thread. The thread end must now be secured as in 'Finishing Off a Thread End' opposite.

Finishing off a Thread End

You will need to finish off a thread end neatly and securely.

Pass the needle through a few beads of the pattern. At that position pick up the thread between the beads with the point of the needle. Pull the needle through to leave a loop of thread 2cm in diameter. Pass the needle through the loop twice (fig 3) and gently pull down to form a double knot between the beads.

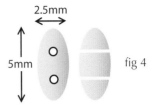

fig 3

Pass the needle through five or six beads of the work and repeat the double knot. Pass the needle through five or six more beads before trimming the thread end as close as possible to the work.

Do not finish off any thread ends until instructed to do so - you might need that thread end again or the needle might have to pass past that position again. See 'Knotty Problems' below.

Knotty Problems

Knots as Obstacles

Be careful where you tie your knots when adding a new thread to your work or finishing off an old thread end. Do not position the knots adjacent to, or inside beads that you have to pass the needle through again, because it will not fit through a hole blocked with thread. Sometimes it is better to leave an old thread end hanging loose and return to it later, than to place a knot where it might cause an obstruction.

Preventing Unwanted Knots

It can be very frustrating to get a knot in your working thread - especially if it keeps happening. There are a few things you can try that might help to prevent these annoying knots.

Don't work with a thread that is too long for you – if the stated 1.8m is too much for you to manage, use a shorter length and add a new thread if necessary.

If you get a knot, undo it carefully and condition the thread, with a suitable product such as Thread Heaven, to remove the distortions in the fibres. The thread will be less likely to re-knot in the same place.

Towards the end of a reel, the thread can be very curly. Cut a slightly shorter length of thread, pulling it between your fingers to help to release the curls, before you prepare the needle. An application of thread conditioner can help too. If it is very distorted be prepared to throw away the last metre or so, rather than spoil your project.

Twin Beads

Twin beads have two parallel holes (fig 4). It is important to thread through the right hole in the correct direction.

2.5mm

5mm

fig 4

Having an eliptical profile, the Twin beads will form a curve if threaded one against the other through the hole at one end (fig 5).

fig 5   fig 6

If you are instructed to pass through the second hole in a Twin bead you must ensure that the needle passes through this hole in the opposite direction creating a strap of thread on the side of the Twin bead (fig 6). This reverses the direction of the needle and gives you access to the outer row of holes on the Twin beads of the previous row.

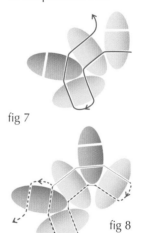

fig 7

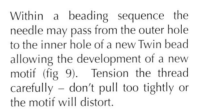

fig 8

Adding a new Twin bead into the gap between the second, or outer holes, on the new row fills in the gap between the outer holes on the first row of Twin beads (fig 7).

You may have to take a long route back to reposition the needle.
Make sure it is pointing in the correct direction for the next row (fig 8).

Within a beading sequence the needle may pass from the outer hole to the inner hole of a new Twin bead allowing the development of a new motif (fig 9). Tension the thread carefully – don't pull too tightly or the motif will distort.

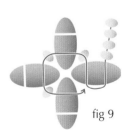

fig 9

Beadwork Stitches for Beginners

There are four basic beadwork stitches used in this book - Ladder stitch, Brick stitch, Square stitch and Herringbone stitch. Ladder stitch can be used to form a foundation row for both Brick stitch and Herringbone stitch so a simple guide to this is given first. Brick stitch features in the Wise Owl Bauble project, Herringbone stitch in the Christmas Stocking Earrings and Square stitch is used in several designs. If you have not used these techniques before you may find these extra notes useful.

Ladder Stitch

Ladder stitch lines up the bead holes in each new stitch parallel to the holes in the previous stitch.

1 Prepare the needle with 1m of single thread and tie a keeper bead 15cm from the end. Thread on two beads. Pass the needle back down through the first bead and up through the second to bring the two beads alongside one another (fig 1).

 fig 1   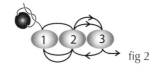 fig 2   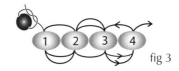 fig 3

2 Thread on a third bead; pass the needle back up bead 2 and back down bead 3 bringing bead 3 to sit alongside beads 1 and 2 (fig 2).
Repeat to add a fourth bead (fig 3). Notice that the thread path alternates up and down with each new stitch. This is Ladder stitch.

In the Christmas Stocking Earrings pattern the beads are added in groups of four. You can see the ladder effect more clearly as each stitch of four beads adds one rung to the Ladder stitch row.

Brick Stitch

Brick stitch is so called because of the pattern the beads form as they line up, in staggered rows, giving the impression of a brick wall. It requires a starter row or 'foundation row' onto which the first row of Brick stitch is worked.

3 The Ladder Stitch Foundation Row - Make a row of ten Ladder-stitched beads as in Steps 1 and 2 (fig 4). The Brick stitches attach to the loops of thread along the edge of the Ladder-stitched row.

fig 4

4 Starting Brick Stitch - Thread on two beads (11 & 12). Pick up the loop of thread between beads 10 and 9 and pass back up through bead 12 in the opposite direction (fig 5). This should bring the two new beads to sit alongside one another with bead 11 slightly overhanging the previous row.

fig 5 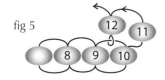   fig 6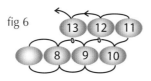

5 Thread on bead 13. Pick up the loop of thread between beads 9 and 8 and pass back up bead 13 (fig 6). Repeat, adding one bead at a time, to the end of the row (ten beads in total).

6 Thread on beads 21 and 22 to start the next row (fig 7) and work to the end of the row.

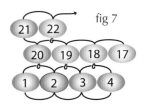
fig 7

This is Brick stitch.

Each row starts with a two-bead stitch followed by a series of single-bead stitches. The beads of each row should sit alongside one another, with the holes parallel and the rows should sit closely on top of one another. You should not be able to see the thread except at the top and bottom of the work.

In the Wise Owl Bauble the eye discs are made in circular Brick stitch around a central 6mm bead.

A strap of thread around the 6mm bead is used as a foundation for the first row of Brick stitch.

The Christmas Stocking Earrings are made using tubular Herringbone stitch.

Herringbone Stitch

Herringbone stitch adds two beads at a time so it grows quite quickly. The thread path pulls the two-bead stitch into a shallow V and as the rows build you start to see a Herringbone (chevron) pattern emerge.

A block of Herringbone stitch needs a foundation row – this is normally made in Ladder stitch. Making the foundation row into a ring creates a circular base for tubular Herringbone stitch.

7 The Ladder Stitch Foundation - Make a row of sixteen Ladder-stitched beads (as in Steps 1 and 2).

Link the first bead to the last with a Ladder stitch to make a ring (fig 8).

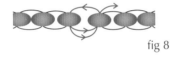

fig 8

To make the first row of tubular Herringbone stitch the needle passes up and down through the holes of the foundation row.

8 Tubular Herringbone Stitch - Thread on two beads. Pass down the next bead around the foundation row and up the following bead (fig 9).

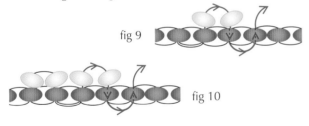

fig 9

fig 10

Thread on two beads. Pass down the next bead around the foundation row and up the following bead (fig 10). Repeat to the end of the row.

Reposition the needle for the next row by passing up through the first bead of the row just completed (fig 11).

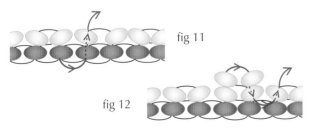

fig 11

fig 12

9 Thread on two beads to start a new row. Pass down through the adjacent bead of the previous row and up through the next bead along (fig 12). Repeat to the end of the row. The Herringbone pattern will begin to show.

Square Stitch

In Square stitch the needle makes a square-shaped path through a newly-added bead and the adjacent bead on the previous row. The Christmas Present Earrings are made from a block of Square-stitched Delica beads.

To begin a block of Square stitch you need a starter row of beads (fig 13).

fig 13

Thread on the first bead of the second row.
Pass the needle back through the last bead of the starter row to bring the new bead alongside this bead with the holes parallel (fig 14).

fig 14   fig 15

Pass the needle through the new bead to complete the Square stitch (fig 15).

Thread on a new bead and pass the needle through the next bead along the starter row and back through the new bead (fig 16) – note the square path of the thread.

fig 16   fig 17

At the end of a row, pass the needle through the previous row and back along the new row to bring all of the beads into line (fig 17).

Square stitch can be shaped to fit a form by increasing or decreasing the bead count. The outer edge of the Wise Owl eye discs is completed with a neatly increased Square stitch row.

To increase within a row, thread on two beads instead of one bead. The needle passes through the second new bead to complete the stitch (fig 18).

fig 18

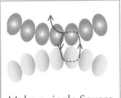

Make a single Square stitch to link two adjacent rows.

Cygnus Bauble

You Will Need

Materials

to make a Red Cygnus Bauble

One 30mm frosted red glass bauble
6g of size 10/0 silver lined gold seed beads A
5g of size 8/0 silver lined red seed beads B
4g of size 3 silver lined red bugle beads C
Five 7mm frost gold two-hole tile beads D
Ten 6mm red fire polished faceted beads E
One 8mm red fire polished faceted bead F
Gold size D beading thread

to make a Gold Cygnus Bauble

One 30mm frosted gold glass bauble
6g of size 10/0 silver lined gold seed beads A
5g of size 8/0 silver lined gold seed beads B
4g of size 3 silver lined gold bugle beads C
Five 7mm frost gold two-hole tile beads D
Ten 6mm topaz fire polished faceted beads E
One 8mm topaz fire polished faceted bead F
Gold size D beading thread

Tools

A size 10 beading needle
A pair of scissors to trim the threads

Simplicity and elegance are the themes for the Cygnus Bauble. The bonus is, it's a quick and easy design to make too. If you have not made a beaded bauble before, start with this one.

The Decoration is Made in Four Stages

A foundation row is fitted around the neck of the bauble.

The long fringe strands, which incorporate the tile beads, are added to the ring of beads.

The swags are added to the tile beads.

The hanging loop is added to the top of the bauble.

1 The Foundation Row - Prepare the needle with 1.5m of single thread and tie a keeper bead 15cm from the end.

2 Thread on five repeats of 1B and 4A. Pass the needle through the first B bead again to bring the beads into a ring (fig 1).

fig 1

fig 2

Place the ring over the neck of the bauble - it needs to fit snugly so you may need to adjust the bead count.

If you need to make an adjustment, add or subtract A beads equally from all five sections to keep the B beads evenly spaced around the ring.

Pass the needle through the beads of the ring once more to make it firm. Finish with the needle emerging from a B bead (as fig 2).

Remove the ring from the bauble.

Extra Info....

Tile beads have two parallel holes. It is important to pass the needle through the correct hole, so follow the diagrams carefully.

In this design there is a fringe strand from each hole on each tile bead.
The first strand is completed before the needle passes down the second parallel hole to start the second strand. This leaves a strap of thread along the top edge of the tile so it's important to choose a thread colour to blend with the tile.

3 The Fringe Strands - Thread on 1A, 1B, 1A, 1C, 1A, 1B, 1A, 1D, 1A, 1B, 1A, 1C, 7A, 1C, 1A, 1B, 1A, 1C, 1A, 1B, 1A, 1E, 1A, 1B and 3A.

Leaving aside the last 3A to anchor the strand, pass the needle back up through the last B bead threaded (fig 3).

fig 3

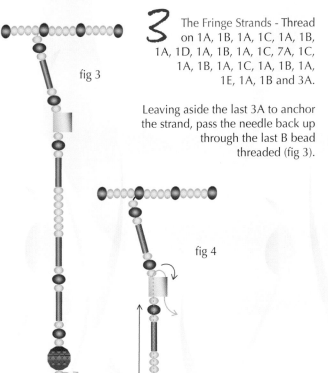

fig 4

4 Pass the needle back up the following beads to emerge from the top of the same hole on the D bead.

Pass the needle down the other hole in the D bead (fig 4).

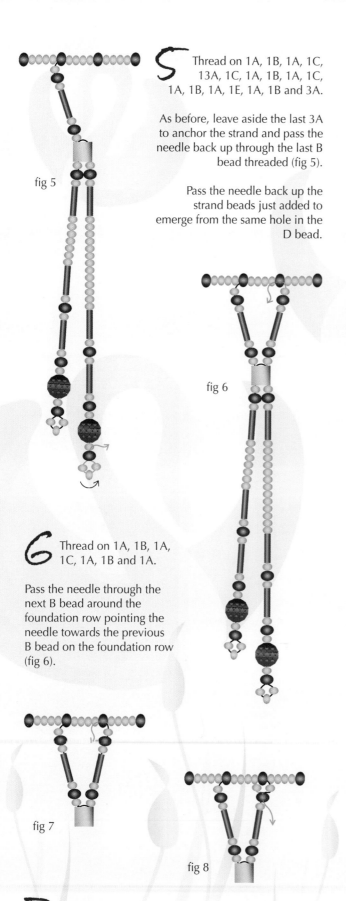

5 Thread on 1A, 1B, 1A, 1C, 13A, 1C, 1A, 1B, 1A, 1C, 1A, 1B, 1A, 1E, 1A, 1B and 3A.

As before, leave aside the last 3A to anchor the strand and pass the needle back up through the last B bead threaded (fig 5).

Pass the needle back up the strand beads just added to emerge from the same hole in the D bead.

fig 5

fig 6

6 Thread on 1A, 1B, 1A, 1C, 1A, 1B and 1A.

Pass the needle through the next B bead around the foundation row pointing the needle towards the previous B bead on the foundation row (fig 6).

fig 7

fig 8

fig 9

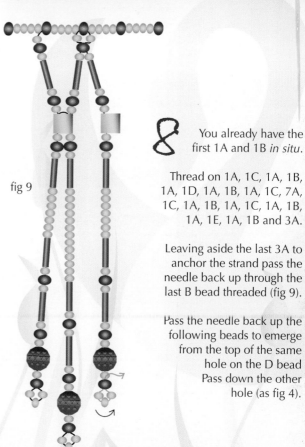

8 You already have the first 1A and 1B *in situ*.

Thread on 1A, 1C, 1A, 1B, 1A, 1D, 1A, 1B, 1A, 1C, 7A, 1C, 1A, 1B, 1A, 1C, 1A, 1B, 1A, 1E, 1A, 1B and 3A.

Leaving aside the last 3A to anchor the strand pass the needle back up through the last B bead threaded (fig 9).

Pass the needle back up the following beads to emerge from the top of the same hole on the D bead Pass down the other hole (as fig 4).

7 Fig 7 shows a close view of the current position of the needle.

Following fig 8 thread on 1A and pass the needle down though the B bead on the previous strand. You are now in the correct place to start to string the next section.

Repeat Steps 5 and 6 to complete the second dangling strand from this D bead and make the connection back to the foundation row around the neck of the bauble.

Repeat Step 7 to start the next section.

Repeat Step 8 and Steps 5 to 7.
Repeat these three steps again to complete eight strands in total.

9
Repeat Step 8 and Step 5.

Thread on 1A, 1B, 1A, 1C and 1A.

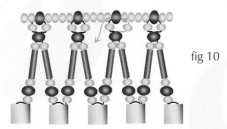

Pass the needle up through the first B bead from Step 3 and thread on 1A. Pass the needle through the B bead on the foundation row (fig 10).

fig 10

10
The Swags - Before you start the swags you need to reposition the needle.

Pass it down through the beads of the last stitch made, to emerge from the D bead above the last fringe strand (fig 11).

fig 11

11
Thread on 8A, 1B, 1A, 1B, 1A, 1B and 8A.

Referring to fig 12 throughout pass the needle up through the first hole on the next D bead around the bauble.

Pass the needle down through the second hole of the same D bead.

Repeat (fig 12).

fig 12

Repeat to make three more swags to link all the D beads together.

Remove the keeper bead and finish off both thread ends neatly and securely.

fig 13

12
The Hanging Loop - Prepare the needle with 1m of single thread and tie a keeper bead 15cm from the end as in Step 1.

Thread on 1B, 1F and 1B. Pass the needle through the loop at the top of the bauble. Pass the needle back up through the beads just added to emerge alongside the keeper bead (fig 13).

Thread on 1A, 2B and 50A.

Pass the needle back down the 2B and the following 1A to pull the 50A up into a loop (fig 14).

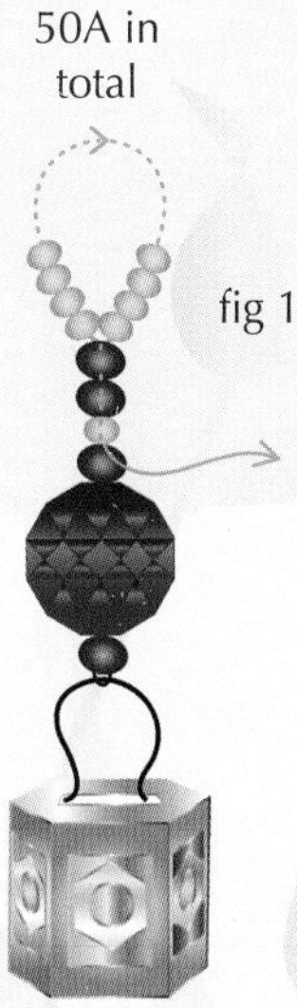

50A in total

fig 14

13
Pass the needle down through the 1B, 1F and 1B and through the bauble loop again. Pass back up through the three beads to the keeper bead.

This second pass of thread has strengthened the connection to the bauble.

Pass the needle back through the 1A, 2B and the 50A of the loop bringing the needle back to the keeper bead.

Repeat Step 13 once more and finish off both thread ends neatly and securely.

Perseus Bauble

You Will Need

Materials

to make the Silver Perseus Bauble

One 40mm silver frost glass bauble
11g of size 10/0 silver lined crystal seed beads A
8g of size 8/0 silver lined crystal seed beads B
7g of size 3 silver lined crystal bugle beads C
Seventeen 7mm pearl white two-hole tile beads D
Sixteen 6mm clear AB fire polished faceted beads E
Sixteen 4mm clear AB fire polished faceted beads F
One 8mm clear fire polished faceted bead G
White size D beading thread

to make the Blue Perseus Bauble

One 40mm blue frost glass bauble
11g of size 10/0 silver lined crystal seed beads A
8g of size 8/0 silver lined blue seed beads B
7g of size 3 silver lined blue bugle beads C
Seventeen 7mm pearl white two-hole tile beads D
Sixteen 6mm pale blue AB fire polished faceted beads E
Sixteen 4mm pale blue AB fire polished faceted beads F
One 8mm pale blue AB fire polished faceted bead G
White size D beading thread

Tools

A size 10 beading needle
A pair of scissors to trim the threads

Two rows of tile beads means this is a step-up in difficulty from the Cygnus Bauble, however it's still a suitable beginners' project. For experienced beaders this is a quick make with a stylish result to repeat time and time again.

The Decoration is Made in Three Stages

A foundation row is fitted around the neck of the bauble.

The long fringe strands, which incorporate the two rows of tile beads, are added to the ring of beads.

The hanging loop is added to the top of the bauble.

1 The Foundation Row - Prepare the needle with 1.5m of single thread and tie a keeper bead 15cm from the end.

2 Thread on eight repeats of 1B and 2A. Pass the needle through the first B bead again to bring the beads into a ring (fig 1).

fig 1

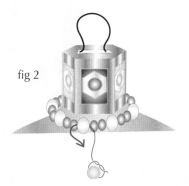

fig 2

Place the ring over the neck of the bauble - it needs to fit snugly so you may need to adjust the bead count.

If you need to make an adjustment, add or subtract A beads equally from all eight sections to keep the B beads evenly spaced around the ring.

Pass the needle through the beads of the ring once more to make it firm. Finish with the needle emerging from a B bead (as fig 2).

Remove the ring from the bauble.

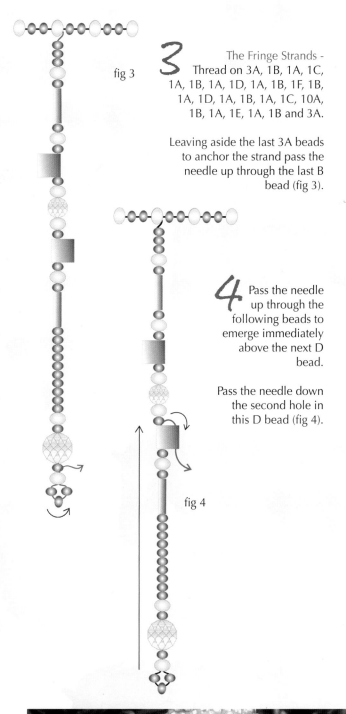

fig 3

3 The Fringe Strands - Thread on 3A, 1B, 1A, 1C, 1A, 1B, 1A, 1D, 1A, 1B, 1F, 1B, 1A, 1D, 1A, 1B, 1A, 1C, 10A, 1B, 1A, 1E, 1A, 1B and 3A.

Leaving aside the last 3A beads to anchor the strand pass the needle up through the last B bead (fig 3).

4 Pass the needle up through the following beads to emerge immediately above the next D bead.

Pass the needle down the second hole in this D bead (fig 4).

fig 4

Extra Info....

Tile beads have two parallel holes. It is important to pass the needle through the correct hole, so follow the diagrams carefully.

In this design the upper row of tiles supports the lower row of tiles. On the lower row each tile supports two strands - one from each hole with the thread passing along the top edge of the tiles to move from one strand to the other.

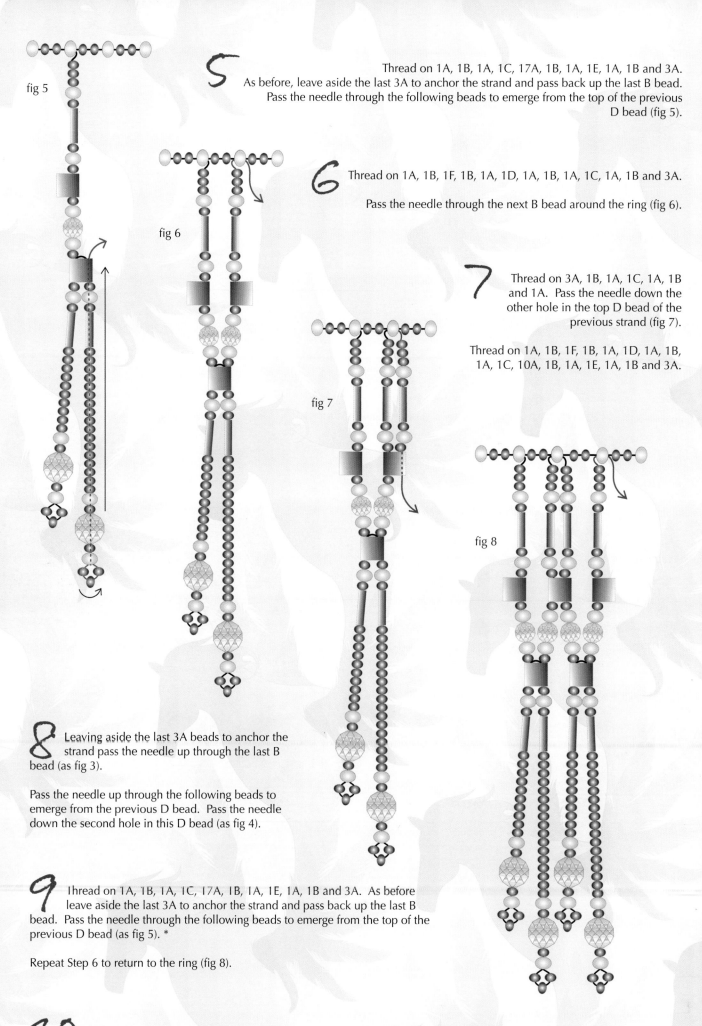

fig 5

5 Thread on 1A, 1B, 1A, 1C, 17A, 1B, 1A, 1E, 1A, 1B and 3A. As before, leave aside the last 3A to anchor the strand and pass back up the last B bead. Pass the needle through the following beads to emerge from the top of the previous D bead (fig 5).

6 Thread on 1A, 1B, 1F, 1B, 1A, 1D, 1A, 1B, 1A, 1C, 1A, 1B and 3A.

Pass the needle through the next B bead around the ring (fig 6).

fig 6

7 Thread on 3A, 1B, 1A, 1C, 1A, 1B and 1A. Pass the needle down the other hole in the top D bead of the previous strand (fig 7).

Thread on 1A, 1B, 1F, 1B, 1A, 1D, 1A, 1B, 1A, 1C, 10A, 1B, 1A, 1E, 1A, 1B and 3A.

fig 7

fig 8

8 Leaving aside the last 3A beads to anchor the strand pass the needle up through the last B bead (as fig 3).

Pass the needle up through the following beads to emerge from the previous D bead. Pass the needle down the second hole in this D bead (as fig 4).

9 Thread on 1A, 1B, 1A, 1C, 17A, 1B, 1A, 1E, 1A, 1B and 3A. As before leave aside the last 3A to anchor the strand and pass back up the last B bead. Pass the needle through the following beads to emerge from the top of the previous D bead (as fig 5). *

Repeat Step 6 to return to the ring (fig 8).

10 Repeat Steps 7, 8 and 9 five more times - this will leave one more set of strands to make.

11

The final set of strands links to the previous D bead (as on the previous repeats) and the first D bead of the first set of strands around the bauble.

Work Steps 7 and 8.
Work to the * in Step 9.
The needle should be emerging from the top of the last D bead.

Thread on 1A, 1B, 1F, 1B and 1A. Pass the needle up through the first D bead of the first strand and thread on 1A, 1B, 1A, 1C, 1A, 1B and 3A.

Pass the needle through the first B bead of the foundation row (fig 9).

Remove the keeper bead and finish off both thread ends neatly and securely.

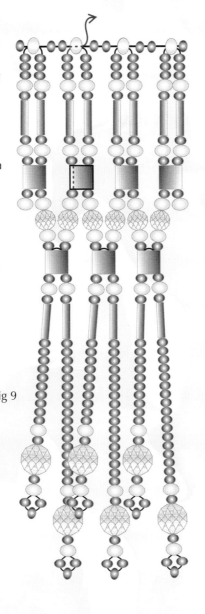

fig 9

fig 10

50A total

fig 11

12

The Hanging Loop - Prepare the needle with 1m of single thread and tie a keeper bead 15cm from the end as in Step 1.

Thread on 1G, 1B, 1A and 1B. Pass the needle through the loop at the top of the bauble and back up the beads just added to emerge alongside the keeper bead (fig 10).

Thread on 1B, 2A, 1D, 1A, 1B, 50A, 1B and 1A. Pass the needle down the other hole in the D bead to draw the last 54 beads into a loop (fig 11).

Thread on 2A and pass down through the B bead above the G bead and the following G bead (fig 12).

Pass the needle through all of the beads twice more – pay particular attention to the stitch through the bauble loop to make the hanging loop strong and durable.

Finish off both thread ends neatly and securely to complete the design.

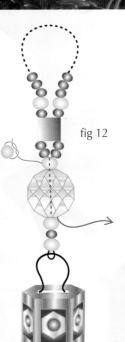

fig 12

Seraphim Angel

✦ ✦

You Will Need

Materials

to make a silver Seraphim Angel

3g of size 10/0 silver lined crystal seed beads A
2g of size 2 crystal bugle beads B
4g of size 10/0 frosted crystal seed beads C
Seven 4mm crystal fire polished faceted beads D
One 8mm crystal fire polished faceted bead E
One 6mm crystal fire polished faceted bead F
White size D beading thread

for the gold Seraphim Angel replace

A with silver lined gold crystal seed beads
and use a golden yellow beading thread

Tools

A size 10 beading needle
A pair of scissors to trim the threads

a Seraphim Angel measures 8cm x 5.5cm
including the hanging loop

An angellic chorus can be yours. These small angel tassels are quite quick to assemble, so you can make a complete choir. Use them for tree decorations, card toppers or gift tags on exquisitely - wrapped presents.

The Decoration is Made in Three Stages

The first wing is made on one the side of the body bead.

The second wing is made on the other side of the body bead.

The head and hanging loop are made next.

The tassel strands of the skirt are added to complete the design.

1 The First Wing - Prepare the needle with 1.2m of single thread and tie a keeper bead 15cm from the end.

Thread on 1E, 1A, 1B and 4A.

Pass the needle through the E bead again to bring the beads into a strap on the side (fig 1).

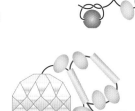
fig 1

2 Before you start the next stitch you need to reposition the needle.

Pass the needle through the first 1A and 1B beads (fig 2).

fig 2

Thread on 2A, 1B and 1A. Pass the needle through the previous B bead to make an oblong stitch (fig 3).

fig 3

fig 4

Reposition the needle for the next stitch by passing through the following 2A and 1B of the new stitch (fig 4).

3 Thread on 1A, 1B and 2A.

Pass up through the previous B bead to make the oblong stitch.

Pass through the following 1A and 1B to reposition the needle (fig 5).

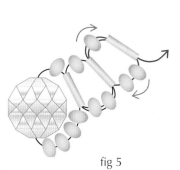
fig 5

fig 6

4 Thread on 2A, 1B and 1A.

Make the stitch as before and reposition the needle through the 2A and 1B ready to make the next stitch (fig 6).

fig 7

Thread on 1A, 1B and 2A for the next stitch and reposition the needle ready for the next stitch (fig 7).

5 Make the next stitch with 2A, 1B and 1A.

Reposition the needle as before (fig 8).

You have completed the top row of the wing.

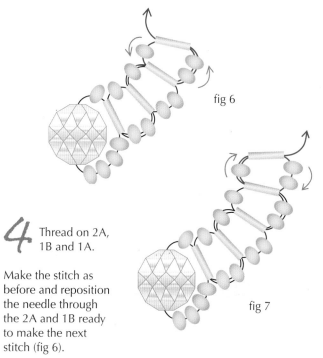

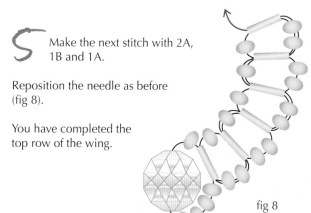
fig 8

6 Pass the needle through the following 1A, 1B and 2A to emerge at the top corner of the first row (fig 9).

fig 9

Thread on 1B, 5A and 1B.

Pass the needle through the last 2A along the edge of the first row (fig 10).

fig 10

Pass the needle through the new beads again and the next 2A along the first row of the wing (fig 11).

fig 11

fig 12

7 Thread on 1B and 4A.

Following fig 12 pass the needle through the B bead of the previous stitch, the 2A along the edge of the first row and the new B bead.

fig 13

8 Thread on 3A and 1B.

Pass through the next 2A along the first row, through the previous B bead, the 3A just added and the new 1B (fig 13).

Pass the needle through the 2A beads outlined in red on fig 13 ready for the next stitch.

9 Thread on 1B and 3A.

Pass the needle through the previous 1B and the 2A of the first row once more (fig 14).

fig 14

Referring to fig 15 thread on 1A (shown in blue) and pass through the next 6A along the edge of the first row. Pass up through the E bead (fig 15).

You now need to pass back along the wing to add in a few extra A beads - this will fill in the gaps and help to stiffen the wing.

fig 15

fig 16

10 Fig 16 shows the A beads you need to add in dark blue.

Pass the needle through the first A bead along the top edge of the wing and thread on 1A. Pass through the next A bead along pulling the new A bead into the gap. Repeat four more times.

Pass through the end B bead and the following 2A of the first row.

Thread on 1A and pass through the next 2A. Push the new A bead into the hole between the B beads and pull the thread firmly. Repeat twice more.

Pass the needle through the last 7A beads of the row and up through the E bead (fig 16).

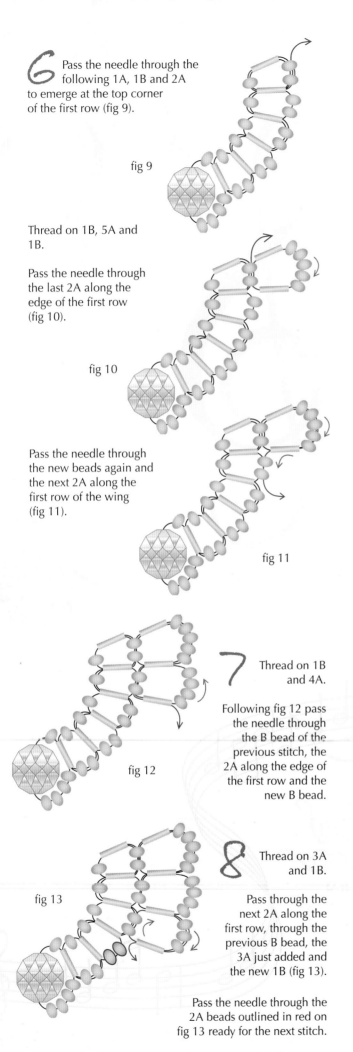

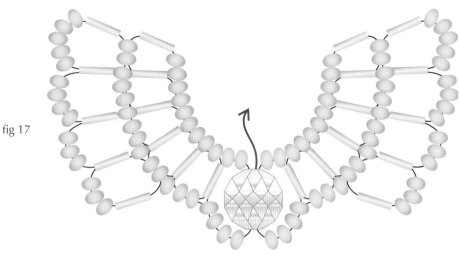

fig 17

11 The Second Wing -
Thread on 1A, 1B and 4A.

Pass up through the E bead to make the first stitch
(as in fig 1).

Repeat from Step 2 to Step 10 to complete this wing.

The needle should be emerging from the top of the E
bead when you finish (fig 17).

12 The Head & Loop
- Thread on 1C,
1F, 1A, 2C and 30A.

Pass the needle back down
the 2C, 1A, 1F, 1C and 1E
beads to draw the 30A into a
loop (fig 18).

30A in total

fig 18

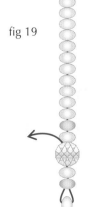

fig 19

13 The Tassel
Strand Skirt -
Thread on 20C, 1A, 1C,
1D, 1C, 1A and 1C.

Leaving aside the last 1C
bead to anchor the strand
pass the needle back up
the last 1A, 1C and 1D
beads (fig 19).

fig 20

14 Pass the needle up through the remaining 22 beads of the strand to emerge just below the E bead. Pass the needle up through the E bead (fig 20).

If necessary adjust the tension in the thread so the tassel strand falls softly from the underside of the E bead but no thread shows between the beads.

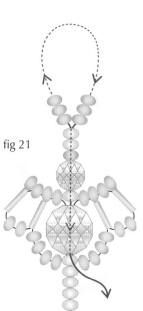

fig 21

15 Pass up the following five beads to emerge at the base of the loop.

Pass through the 30A beads of the loop and back down through the head and body to emerge at the top of the previous tassel strand ready to make the next strand of the skirt (fig 21).

Repeat Steps 13 and 14 to make the second tassel strand.

Repeat Step 15 to reposition the needle for the next strand.

Repeat until you have completed seven tassel strands in total. If you find it is getting difficult to pass the needle through the A and C beads above the head: read the Extra Info box opposite.

16 If the needle will fit through the beads, reinforce the wings by passing through the route shown in fig 16, on both wings.

Finish off all the remaining thread ends neatly and securely.

Extra Info....

As you pass up and down through the body beads, and the 30A beads of the loop, the holes become filled with thread. You may find that the needle won't pass through enough times to make all seven tassel strands.

fig 22

If this happens bring the thread back to the top of the last tassel strand.

Make a loop of thread around the base of the E bead immediately above the top beads of the strands.

Pass the needle through the loop and pull to form a knot against the underside of the E bead (fig 22).

You can now make the next tassel strand straight away.

17 Your angel should now be ready to display. If the wings are a little soft, or tend to curl over at the ends you can stiffen them with a little clear nail varnish.

Stiffening the Wings - Working in a well-ventilated space lay the angel out flat on a piece of polythene.

Paint a very thin coat of clear nail varnish onto the wings paying particular attention to the top and middle rows of A beads. Do not get the varnish onto the C beads as it will spoil the matt finish on these beads. The nail varnish will trickle between the beads and stiffen the threads. Leave to dry completely. Flip the angel over and repeat.

Repeat at least once more on each side. It is better to build up two thin coats than make one thick application, so take your time.

Vela Star

You Will Need

Materials

to make a Silver Vela Star

6g of size 8/0 silver lined crystal seed beads A
6g of size 3 silver lined crystal bugle beads B
3g of size 10/0 silver lined crystal seed beads C
Eight 6mm crystal fire polished faceted beads D
Seven 4mm crystal fire polished faceted beads E
One 12mm crystal fire polished faceted bead F
White size D beading thread

to make a Gold Vela Star

Swap A, B and C for silver lined gold
seed beads and bugles.
Keep the crystal fire polished faceted beads.
Swap the white thread for gold.

Tools

A size 10 beading needle
A pair of scissors to trim the threads

a Vela Star measures 9cm x 6cm including the
hanging loop

Perfectly-proportioned star points surround a large faceted central bead for maximum sparkle. This is a classic design that you will want to use again and again.

The Decoration is Made in Three Stages

A Ladder-stitched cylinder of beads is made first.

The star points are added, one at a time, around the cylinder.

The final stage places the F bead in the centre and makes the hanging loop at the top.

1 The Cylinder - Prepare the needle with 1.5m of single thread and tie a keeper bead 15cm from the end.

Thread on 2A, 1C, 2A and 1C.

Pass the needle through the first 2A to make an oblong (fig 1).

Pass the needle through the following 1C and 2A (fig 2).

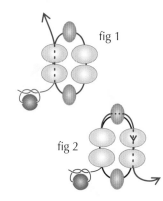

fig 1

fig 2

2 Thread on 1C, 2A and 1C. Pass the needle through the previous 2A and the following new 1C and 2A to make a second oblong (fig 3).

Repeat Step 2 (fig 4).

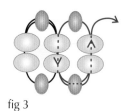

fig 3

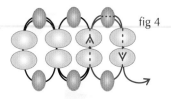

fig 4

Repeat Step 2 a further ten times until you have a Ladder stitch strip of thirteen linked oblongs (14 x 2A ladder rungs).

3 You now need to join the two ends of the strip together.

Thread on 1C. Bring the strip around into a cylinder shape and pass through the first 2A of the first stitch. Thread on 1C and pass through the last 2A of the last stitch (fig 5).

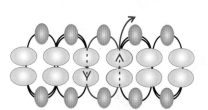

fig 5

4 Pass through the first C bead along the adjacent edge and thread on 1C. Pass through the next C bead along. Thread on 1C and pass through the next C bead along (fig 6).

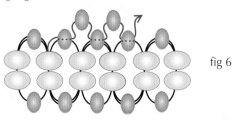

fig 6

Repeat right around this edge of the cylinder to make a continuous row of C beads. Pass the needle through all these C beads once more to make the ring neat.

Pass the needle through the adjacent 2A stitch to the other edge of the cylinder and repeat to make a matching C bead edge.

You should now have a small cylinder of beads.

5 Before you move on, check that 1F will fit into the centre of the ring - it's easier to do the next stage without the F bead in place but if you pull the thread too tightly now it won't fit later in the pattern. Make sure it fits snugly (slackening off the thread through the two edges if it's too tight) and can go in and out easily.

Take the F bead out for now and place to the side.

6 Pass the needle through the adjacent 2A ladder rung (fig 7). The needle is now in the correct position to start the first star point.

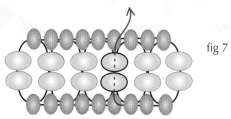

fig 7

8 Reposition the Needle - Fig 10 shows the top view of the work - pass the needle through the next C bead along the edge of the cylinder and the following rung of 2A (fig 10).

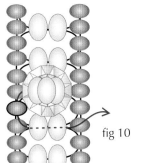

fig 10

9 Bugle Edge One - Thread on 1A, 1B and 2C.

Referring to fig 11 pass the needle up through the E bead on the Central Strut and the following 1C and 1A.

Pass the needle through the 3A beads of the anchor and back down the 1A, 1C and 1E below the anchor (fig 11).

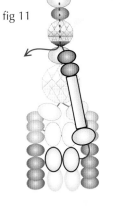

fig 11

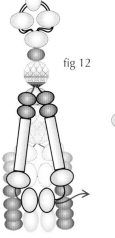

fig 12

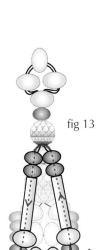

fig 13

7 Making the Star Points - The Central Strut - Thread on 1A, 1D, 1A, 1E, 1C and 4A.

Leaving aside the last 3A beads to anchor the strand pass the needle back through the first 1A of the 4A and the following four beads to emerge below the D bead (fig 8).

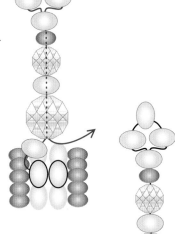

fig 8

fig 9

Thread on 1A and pass through the same 2A beads of the cylinder to bridge the strut across the width of the ladder rung (fig 9).

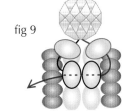

10 Thread on 2C, 1B and 1A. Pass the needle through the same 2A rung on the cylinder (fig 12).

At present the bugles will be very unstable - you need to make two more stitches to make them firm.

Referring to fig 13 pass the needle up through the 1A, 1B and 2C of the first stitch and down the 2C, 1B and 1A of the second stitch.

Pass through the 2A of the rung on the cylinder (fig 13).

11 Referring to fig 14 pass the needle up though the first 1A of this Bugle Edge and thread on 1A.

Pass up through the 1B and lowest 1C of the second stitch (fig 14).

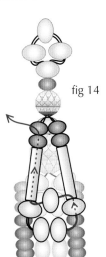

fig 14

12

Referring to fig 15 pass the needle down the adjacent 1C above the other bugle and the B bead that follows.

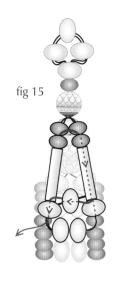

fig 15

Pass the needle through the new A bead link between the bugles and down through the bottom A bead below the second bugle (fig 15).

Pass the needle through the 2A beads of the rung to make the base firm.

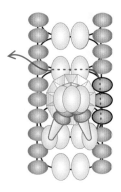

13

Reposition the Needle - Fig 16 shows the top view - pass the needle through the 3C beads alongside the new point and through the 2A of the next vacant rung (adjacent to the far side of the Central Strut) (fig 16).

These 2A support the Second Bugle Edge for this point.

fig 16

14

Bugle Edge Two - Repeat from Step 9 to Step 12 to make the second bugle edge for this point (fig 17).

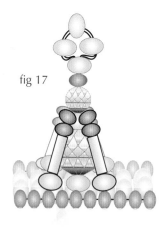

fig 17

Following fig 18 pass the needle through the next C bead along the edge of the cylinder and through the next 2A rung ready to start the next star point (fig 18).

15

Make a Central Strut to bridge the 2A of this rung as in Step 7 (see fig 19).

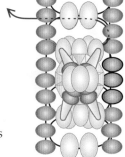

fig 18

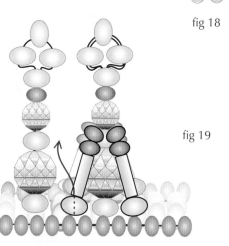

fig 19

Bugle Edge One - This is supported by the 2A beads that also support Bugle Edge Two of the previous point.

Referring to fig 19 pass the needle back through the adjacent C bead on the edge of the cylinder, through the 2A of the rung underneath the previous Bugle Edge and up through the A bead at the base of the first B bead (fig 19).

Fig 19 highlights the 2A of the rung in turquoise and the A bead link added in figs 14 & 15 in orange).

16

Thread on 1B and 2C. Referring to fig 11 pass the needle up the 1E, 1C and 1A beads of the new Central Strut, around the 3A anchor and back down again to emerge just below the E bead (see fig 11).

Thread on 2C and 1B. Pass down through the A bead at the base of the second bugle bead of the previous point and through the 2A of the shared rung on the cylinder (as fig 12).

You have now linked the two bugle edges together but you still need to reinforce the new stitches.

17   Make the first reinforcing stitch on the new point as shown in fig 13.

Pass up through the bottom (shared) A bead of the first Bugle Edge stitch to emerge just below the bugle bead. Pass the needle through the A bead link added in figs 14 and 15.

Make the strengthening stitches up and down the new point as in figs 14 and 15 passing through the existing A bead link again at the base of the bugles.

Pass through the A bead below the second bugle (as fig 15) to complete the reinforcement of the new Bugle Edge on this side of the new Central Strut.

18   Referring to fig 20, pass the needle through the following 3C along the edge of the cylinder.

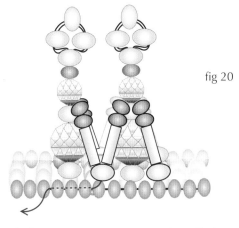

fig 20

Pass through the next vacant 2A rung on the cylinder ready to add the Bugle Edge Two to the new point.

Complete the point as in Step 9 to Step 12.

Reposition the needle for the start of the next Central Strut as in fig 18, and repeat until you have completed all seven star points. When you make the seventh point make sure you link the Bugle Edge Two stitches to the first Bugle Edge One of the first point.

Do not finish off the thread ends yet.

19   The Hanging Loop - Place the F bead back into the centre of the cylinder with the hole running top to bottom of the star. If necessary pass the needle through the C bead rims of the cylinder to tighten it around the F bead so it's snug. If the F bead is still a little loose you can pass the needle through the F bead hole to secure it but this may not be necessary.

If you have a thread length of 50cm or more remaining, keep that for the hanging loop - otherwise finish off all the thread ends neatly and securely.

20   If necessary attach a new 70cm single thread to the work to emerge from the A bead link between the bases of two adjacent points (fig 21 shown in orange).

Thread on 8C, 1A, 1D, 1A and 40C.

Pass the needle back through the last 1A, 1D, 1A and 6C to draw up the loop (fig 21).

40C in total

fig 21

fig 22

Thread on 2C and pass the needle through the A bead link between the bugles in the same direction as before to bridge the base of the strand across the width of the A bead.

Pass the needle back up through the beads just added, around the hanging loop and back down to the star edge to strengthen the connections.

Finish off the thread ends neatly and securely.

 29

Brandy Puddings

✦ ✦

You Will Need

To Make a Small Pudding Bauble

One 30mm frosted brown glass bauble
3g of size 10/0 white lined crystal seed beads A
3g of size 10/0 silver lined green seed beads C
Six 4mm red fire polished faceted beads G
One 6mm red fire polished faceted bead E

To Make a Medium Pudding Bauble

One 40mm frosted brown glass bauble
4g of size 10/0 white lined crystal seed beads A
4g of size 10/0 silver lined green seed beads C
Three 6mm red fire polished faceted beads F
One 8mm red fire polished faceted bead D

To Make a Large Pudding Bauble

One 60mm frosted brown glass bauble
10g of size 10/0 white lined crystal seed beads A
0.5g of size 8/0 white lined crystal seed beads B
10g of size 10/0 silver lined green seed beads C
Six 8mm red fire polished faceted beads D
One 6mm red fire polished faceted beads E
One 12mm crystal fire polished faceted bead F

All pudding sizes require white size D
beading thread: add emerald green for
the large pudding.

Tools

A size 10 beading needle
A pair of scissors to trim the threads

Three sumptuous treats to choose from…and all calorie-free! The small pudding is easy to make but the leaves are small, so take your time. The leaves on the medium pudding have a more detailed outline and the large pudding is smothered with extra brandy sauce. Just keep them hidden from sweet-toothed guests!

The Small Pudding

The Small Pudding is Made in Four Stages
A foundation row to fit the neck of the bauble is made first.

The brandy sauce swags are made and stitched to the foundation row.

The leaves and berries are added.

The hanging loop completes the decoration.

1 The Foundation Row - Prepare the needle with 1.5m of single white thread and tie a keeper bead 15cm from the end.

Thread on 24A and pass the needle through the first A bead to make a ring (fig 1).

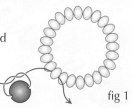

fig 1

2 Place this ring over the neck of the bauble (fig 2).

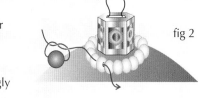

fig 2

The ring needs to fit snugly around the base of the bauble neck without the thread showing between the beads.

If the fit is too tight remove the ring and rethread it with a count of 30A. Check the fit again - you need a number that will divide easily into six sections - if 30 is still too tight try 33A or 36A.

Pass the needle through the A beads of the ring once more to emerge as in fig 2 - this will make the ring more firm and give you a sturdier base to work from. Remove the ring from the bauble - it's easier to work when it's not on the bauble.

Adapt Your Bead Count to Fit the Pattern

If you have a count of 24A you will be working on six sections of 4A.

If you have a count of 30A you will be working on six sections of 5A.

If you have a bead count of 33A you will be working on six alternating sections 5A, 6A, 5A, 6A, 5A and 6A.

If you have a bead count of 36A you will be working on six sections of 6A.

The following diagrams will assume a bead count of 24A around the neck - if you have a different bead count guidance is given where necessary.

3 The Brandy Sauce Swags - Thread on 25A.

For a 4A section- Count 4A back around the ring from the start position. Pass your needle through the first 3A of these beads to form a loop emerging 1A from the start of the loop (fig 3).

For a 5A section - Count 5A back around the ring from the start position. Pass your needle through the first 4A of these beads to form a loop emerging 1A from the start of the loop (as fig 3 but with the loop bridging across 5A of the ring instead of 4A beads).

For a 6A section - Count 6A back around the ring from the start position. Pass your needle through the first 5A of these beads to form a loop emerging 1A from the start of the loop (as fig 3 but with the loop bridging across 6A of the ring instead of 4A beads).

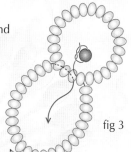

fig 3

4 Thread on 17A.

For a 4A section - Pass the needle through the previous 2A of the ring and the following 5A to emerge 4A from the side of the previous loop (fig 4).

For a 5A section - Pass the needle through the previous 3A of the ring and the following 6A to emerge 5A from the side of the previous loop (see fig 4 for technique only).

For a 6A section - Pass the needle through the previous 4A of the ring and the following 7A to emerge 6A from the side of the previous loop (see fig 4 for technique only).

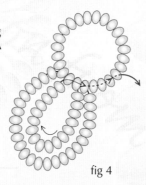

fig 4

5 Thread on 23A.

For a 4A section - Pass the needle through the first 2A of the previous large swag and the following 3A of the ring (fig 5).

For a 5A section - Pass the needle through the first 2A of the previous large swag and the following 4A of the ring (see fig 5 for technique only).

For a 6A section - Pass the needle through the first 2A of the previous large swag and the following 5A of the ring (see fig 5 for technique only).

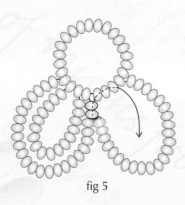

fig 5

Repeat Step 4 to add the smaller swag in the centre of the large swag as before and to move on to the next start position (fig 6).

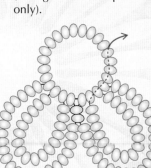

fig 6

6 Repeat Step 5 three more times.

The needle should be emerging alongside the edge of the first large swag.

Pass the needle through the following 2A of this swag (fig 7) and thread on 21A.

Complete the large swag as before and the small swag inside it.

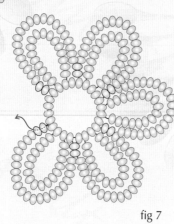

fig 7

7 You have six interlinked double swags around the ring. The swags are now divided into adjacent pairs - each pair will support three leaves and two berries.

Fig 8 shows two adjacent double swags in bold with three green markers for the leaves and two red markers for the berries.

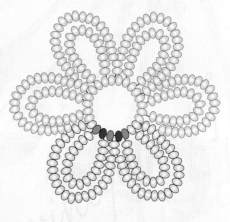

fig 8

If you have worked with 5A or 6A sections you may want to space the leaves and berries out along the ring at the top of the swags just a little - the important thing is to make a leaf, a berry, a leaf, a berry and a leaf.

8 The Leaves & Berries - Pass the needle through the ring beads to emerge from the position you have chosen for the first leaf. You will be making two sizes of leaf - small and large.

Make a Small Leaf - Thread on 9C. Pass the needle back through the 6th, 5th and 4th C beads to pull the last 3C into a picot (fig 9). You now have the tip of the leaf and the central leaf stem.

Thread on 3C. Pass the needle through the 4th C bead on the stem in the same direction to make a picot on the side (fig 10).

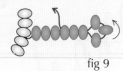

fig 9

Repeat to make a picot on the other side of the stem at this position.

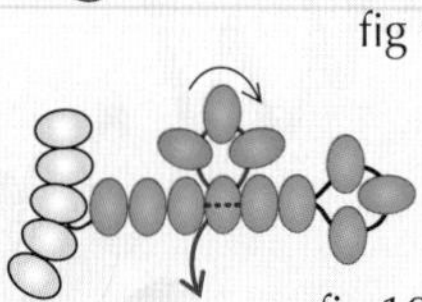

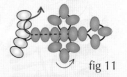

fig 10

Pass the needle through the following 3C beads of the stem to emerge at the ring (fig 11).

fig 11

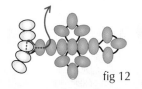

fig 12

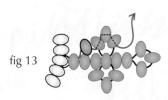

fig 13

fig 14

9 Pass the needle through the A bead of the ring and back through the first bead of the stem (fig 12).

Thread on 1C and pass through the 3C of the first side picot (fig 13).

Thread on 1C and pass through the 3C at the tip of the leaf (fig 14).

Thread on 1C and pass through the 3C of the picot on the other side of the stem.

Thread on 1C and pass through the first 1C of the stem (fig 15) and the following 2A of the ring (fig 16).

Make sure the needle is emerging from the bead that you have chosen to support the first berry.

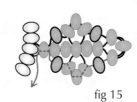

fig 15

fig 16

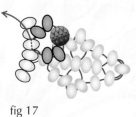

fig 17

10 The Berry - Thread on 2C, 1G and 2C. Pass the needle through the A bead on the ring again to bring the berry up close to the ring (fig 17).

Pass the needle through the next A bead of the ring - if you are following the plan shown in fig 8 this is the correct place for the next leaf. If you have chosen the next bead along, pass the needle through this bead ready to make the next leaf.

11 Make a Large Leaf - This is very similar to the small leaf but with a longer stem. Thread on 11C.

Pass the needle back through the 8th-5th C beads to pull the last 3C into a picot (fig 18).

Add a 3C picot on either side of this C bead and pass through to the start of the stem (fig 19).

Pass the needle through the A bead on the ring and back through the first C bead of the stem (fig 20).

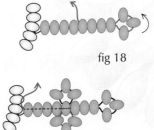

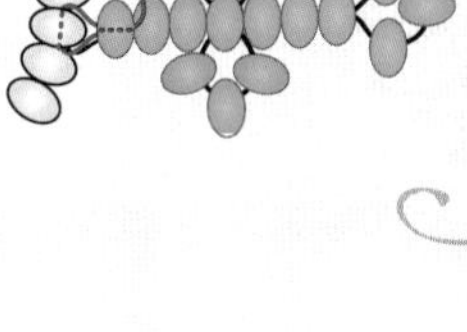

fig 18

fig 19

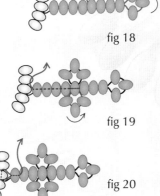

fig 20

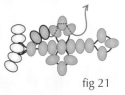

fig 21

12 Thread on 2C and pass through the 3C of the first side picot (fig 21).

Thread on 2C and pass through the 3C picot at the end of the stem (fig 22).

Thread on 1C and pass through the picot on the other side of the stem. Thread on 1C and pass through the first 1C bead of the stem (fig 23). The change of bead count on this side of the leaf makes it twist like a holly leaf.

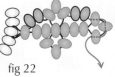

fig 22

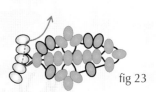

fig 23

Pass through the A bead on the ring and the following 1A (or required number of A beads) ready to add the next berry.

13 Add a berry as before using 3C on either side, instead of 2C, to vary the texture of the work. Pass the needle through to the last leaf position on this cluster and add a small leaf as in Steps 8 and 9.

Pass the needle through the A beads of the ring to the next pair of double swags and add a similar cluster of small leaf, berry, large leaf, berry and small leaf at this position.

Repeat once more to embellish the final pair of swags and finish off the thread ends neatly and securely.

Place the ring back over the bauble arranging the leaves and berries over the top surface of the swags.

14 The Hanging Loop - Prepare the needle with 1m of single white thread and tie a keeper bead 15cm from the end.

Thread on 1C, 1E and 1C. Pass the needle through the metal loop at the top of the bauble and back up through the beads just added (fig 24).

Thread on 1A and 30C. Pass the needle back down through the A bead to draw the 30C into a loop (fig 25).

Pass the needle down through the connection to the bauble loop and up and around the 30C hanging loop twice more to strengthen before finishing off both thread ends neatly and securely.

fig 24

30C in total

fig 25

The Medium Pudding

The Medium Pudding is Made in Four Stages

A foundation row to fit the neck of the bauble is made first.

The brandy sauce swags are added to the foundation row.

The leaves and berries are added.

The hanging loop completes the decoration.

15 The Foundation Row - Following Steps 1 and 2 make a ring of beads to fit the neck of the bauble.

For this design the bead count needs to be easily divisible by six so choose the best fit from 24A, 30A, 36A or 42A. If you need a greater bead count, that is fine, just make sure you can divide it easily into the required six sections.

Adapt Your Bead Count to Fit the Pattern

The following bead counts around the ring assume a total count of 30A around the neck of the bauble. If you have made a count adjustment you will need to make an allowance for the extra beads within each of the six swag sections.

The adjustment for 36A is shown in red brackets for guidance.

16 The Brandy Sauce Swags - Thread on 41A.

Count back 3A around the ring of 30A (36A). Pass the needle through these 3A towards the top of the 41A and the following 5A (6A) around the ring.

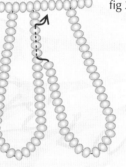

fig 26

fig 27

17 Thread on 35A. Pass the needle through the 6th, 5th, 4th and 3rd A beads of the last swag (fig 27).

Thread on 2A and pass the needle through the 3A before the start of this swag and the following 5A (6A) of the ring (fig 28).

Repeat three more times to make five swags in total.

The last swag needs to link the fifth swag to the first swag.

fig 28

18 Thread on 2A.

Pass the needle through the 39th, 38th, 37th and 36th A beads of the first swag and thread on 29A.

Pass the needle up through the 6th, 5th, 4th and 3rd A beads of the fifth swag and thread on 2A.

Pass the needle through the third A bead (4th) around the ring (fig 29).

fig 29

19 Pass the needle through the next 2A beads of the ring and the first 2A beads of the swag.

Thread on 25A.

Pass the needle up through the 2A beads at the other side of this large swag to complete a medium-sized swag inside the large swag (fig 30).

fig 30

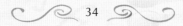

Pass the needle through the following 2A of the ring and thread on 15A.

Pass the needle through the previous 1A bead on the ring to form a small swag inside the other two (fig 31).

fig 31

Pass the needle through the following 4A (5A) beads of the ring.

Repeat Steps 19 and 20 to add a medium and a small swag to each of the large swags.

Leave the needle attached and emerging from one of the A beads of the foundation ring.

21 The Leaves and Berries - There are three clusters, each containing two leaves and a berry, to add to the foundation ring of A beads.

The three clusters will need to be equally spaced around the ring.

Each cluster will occupy three adjacent A beads on the ring.

Trying to avoid any A beads that may have become very full of thread already, select the position for the first cluster. If necessary reposition the needle for the first leaf at your preferred position on the A bead ring.

22 Each leaf has a main stem and four leaf ribs which are linked together to make the distinctive holly leaf shape. You need to pull the thread quite firmly to make the stem and ribs taut.

Thread on 15C.

Leaving aside the last 3C beads threaded to anchor the strand, pass the needle back through the next 4C (fig 32).

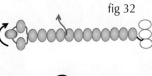
fig 32

Thread on 5C.

Leaving aside the last 3C beads to anchor the strand, pass the needle back through the second and first C beads just added and the C bead on the main stem (fig 33).

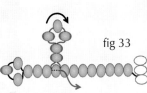
fig 33

Thread on 5C and make a similar leaf rib on the other side of the main stem (fig 34).

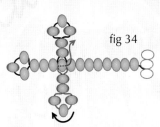
fig 34

Pass the needle through the following 5C beads of the main stem and repeat the leaf ribs on either side of this C bead (fig 35).

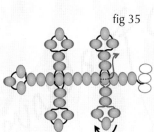
fig 35

23 Pass the needle through the following 2C beads of the stem to emerge between the first and second C beads at the base of the leaf.

Thread on 3C.

Pass the needle through the 3C beads at the end of the last leaf rib made (fig 36).

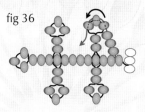
fig 36

Thread on 5C and pass the needle through the 3C beads at the tip of the next rib along. Thread on 2C and pass the needle through the 3C beads at the tip of the leaf stem (fig 37).

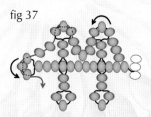
fig 37

Thread on 2C and pass through the 3C at the tip of the following leaf rib and thread on 5C before you pass through the 3C at the tip of the last leaf rib.

Thread on 3C. Pass the needle through the first C bead of the leaf stem to emerge adjacent to the A bead ring.

Pull the thread tight to crinkle the holly leaf and pass the needle through the A bead on the ring at the base of the leaf.

24 Pass the needle through the next bead around the A bead ring to be in the correct position to add the berry.

Thread on 4C, 1E and 4C. Pass the needle through the A bead on the ring to draw the berry into place (fig 38).

fig 38

Pass the needle through the next 1A bead of the ring and thread on 15C to start the second leaf of the pair.

Complete this leaf as before.

Pass the needle through the A beads of the ring to the position you have chosen for the second cluster and make a leaf, a berry and a leaf as in Steps 22 to 24.

Repeat to add the third cluster and finish off the thread ends neatly and securely.

Place the completed ring over the bauble neck arranging the leaves and berries over the top of the brandy sauce swags.

25 The Hanging Loop - Prepare the needle with 1m of single white thread and tie a keeper bead 10cm from the end.

Thread on 1C, 1D and 1C. Pass the needle through the metal loop at the top of the bauble and back up through the beads just added (fig 39).

40C in total

Thread on 1A and 40C. Pass the needle back down through the A bead to draw the 40C into a loop (fig 40).

fig 39

Pass the needle down through the connection to the bauble loop and up and around the 40C hanging loop twice more to strengthen.

Finish off both thread ends neatly and securely.

fig 40

left - frosted silver baubles decorated with silvery swags, pearl white holly leaves and crystal AB berries

The Large Pudding

The Large Pudding is Made in Four Stages

A foundation row to fit the neck of the bauble is made first.

The brandy sauce swags are added to the foundation row.

The leaves and berries are made on a separate ring.

The hanging loop completes the decoration.

26 The Foundation Row - Prepare the needle with 1.5m of single white thread and tie a keeper bead 15cm from the end.

Thread on six repeats of 1B and 3A. Pass the needle through the first B again to bring the beads into a ring (fig 41).

fig 41

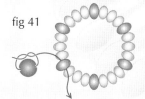

Place the ring over the neck of the bauble - it needs to fit snugly without the thread showing between the beads.

If the fit is not good, remove the ring and rethread with six repeats of 1B and 4A (or 1B and 5A). You need the six B beads to be equally spaced around the bauble neck.

27 Pass the needle through the beads of the circle once more to make the ring firm. Finish with the needle emerging from a B bead (fig 42). Remove the ring from the bauble.

The following diagrams assume a bead count as in fig 41. Any extra A beads you may have added to make the foundation row fit your bauble will be passed through in Steps 28 and 29 (figs 44 and 46) and will not affect the pattern.

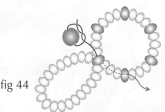

fig 42

28 The Swags - Thread on 20A.

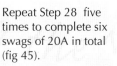

fig 43

Pass the needle through the B bead on the ring in the same direction to draw the new A beads into a loop (fig 43).

Pass through the beads of the ring to emerge from the next B bead around the ring (fig 44).

fig 44

Repeat Step 28 five times to complete six swags of 20A in total (fig 45).

fig 45

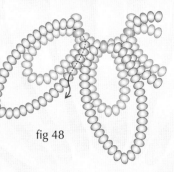

30 Pass through the next 1A bead around the ring and the first 5A beads of the first swag made in Step 29 (fig 48).

fig 48

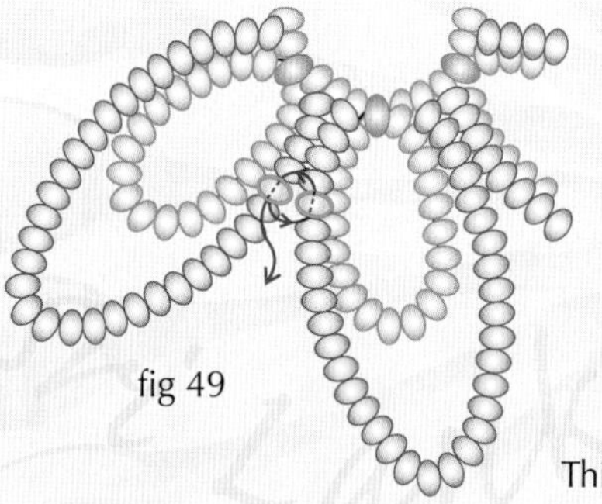

fig 49

Pass the needle up through the corresponding fifth A bead from the top of the adjacent 35A swag and down through the fifth A of the first 35A swag again (fig 49).

This Square stitch has linked the two swags together. Thread on 45A.

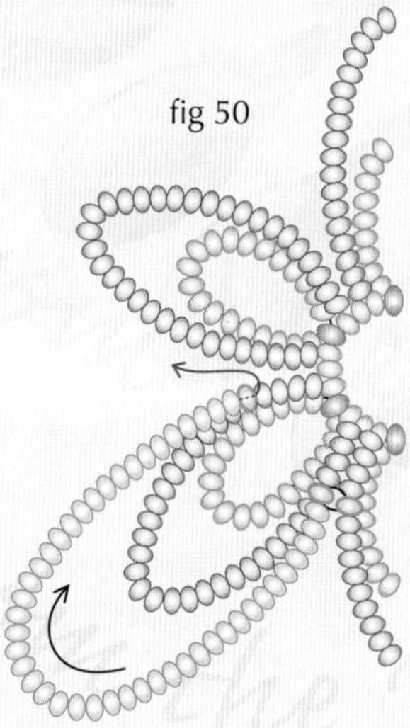

fig 50

31 Pass the needle up through the fifth A bead from the top of the current 35A swag (fig 50). Note - you are now working in the opposite direction around the swags.

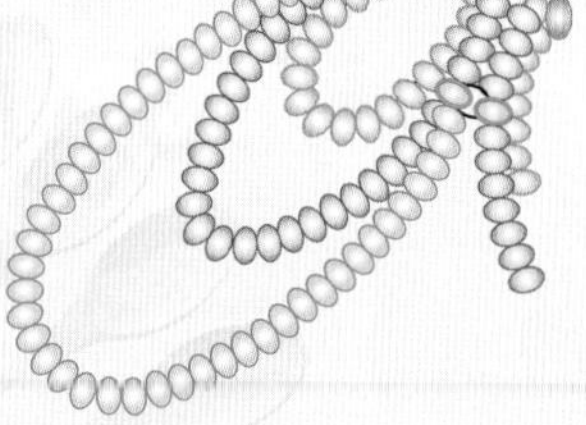

fig 51

fig 52

29 Pass through the next 1A bead around the ring and thread on 35A.

Pass the needle through the A bead before the previous B bead on the ring, the B bead and the following A beads to emerge from the next B bead around the ring (fig 46).

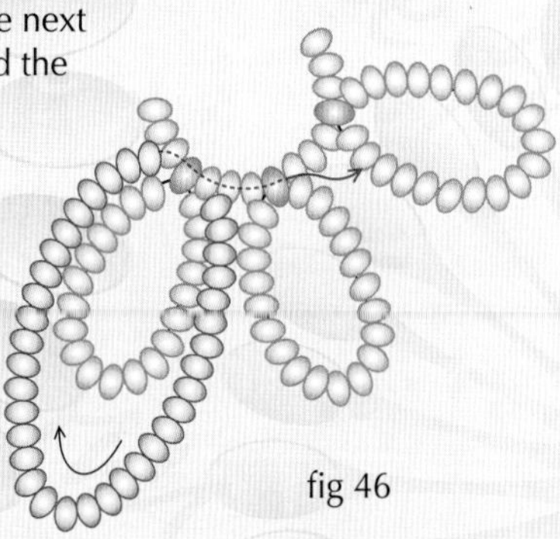

fig 46

Pass the needle down the corresponding fifth A on the adjacent 35A swag, back up the fifth A of the first swag and back down the fifth A on the adjacent swag once more (fig 51). This completes a Square stitch and links the two swags together.

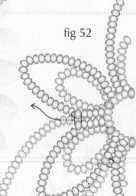

Pass the needle down through the last 2A of the 45A just added (fig 52).

Repeat Step 29 five more times to complete six swags of 35A in total (fig 47).

32 Thread on 43A and repeat Step 31.

Repeat Step 32 three more times to complete five swags. The sixth swag has to be linked to the first swag.

fig 47

33 For the sixth swag thread on 41A (the last 2A are already *in situ* as part of the first swag of 45A).

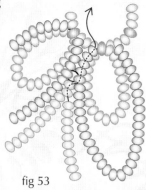

Pass the needle up through the first 2A of the first 45A swag and the following 5A beads to emerge at the ring (fig 53).

fig 53

Remove the keeper bead and finish off both thread ends neatly and securely.

Place the completed set of swags over the bauble neck.

34 Making the Holly Ring - Prepare the needle with 1.5m of single emerald thread and tie a keeper bead 15cm from the end.

Thread on 24C. Pass the needle through the first C bead to make a ring of beads (fig 54).

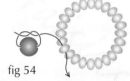

fig 54

As before, check the fit of the ring around the neck of the bauble and adjust the count if necessary. You will need to divide the ring into six sections to support six leaves and six berries. A count of 24C (as shown in fig 54) is easy to divide into six sets of 4C. The following instructions will assume you have a count of 24C - see below for more information about other bead counts.

Pass the needle through the beads of the ring once more to make it a little more firm before you move on. Remove the ring from the bauble.

Adapt Your Bead Count to Fit the Bauble

You need to divide your ring into six sections.

30C divides easily into six sets of 5C.

If you find you have a more awkward count, for example 27C, divide it into alternating blocks of 4C and 5C to spread the extra 3C beads around the ring at regular intervals.

Make a note of your count and the sequence you are going to use - e.g. for a total of 26C a good sequence is 4C, 4C, 5C, 4C, 4C, 5C.

As you work around the ring adding the leaves and berries, keep an eye on your note so you finish with the most even spacing your bead count will allow.

35 The Leaves - As you work each leaf keep the tension in the thread a little more firm than normal - this will help to make the holly spiky.

Thread on 20C.

Leaving aside the last 3C beads to anchor the strand, pass the needle back through the following 5C making a picot at the end of the main stem (fig 55).

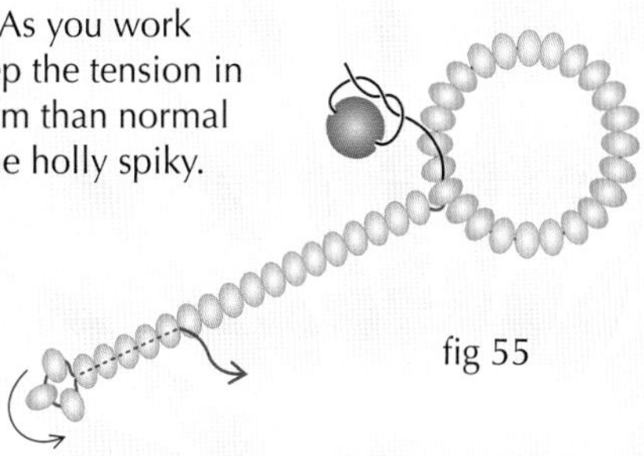

fig 55

36 Thread on 6C.

Leaving aside the last 3C pass the needle back through the first 3C just added.

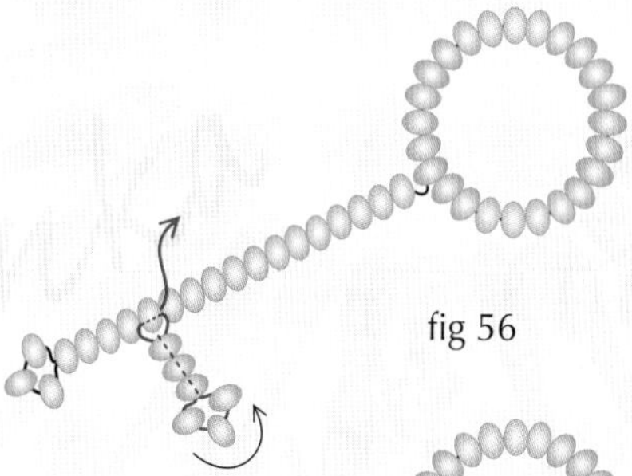

fig 56

Pass the needle through the C bead on the main stem in the same direction to make a leaf rib with a picot at the end as before (fig 56).

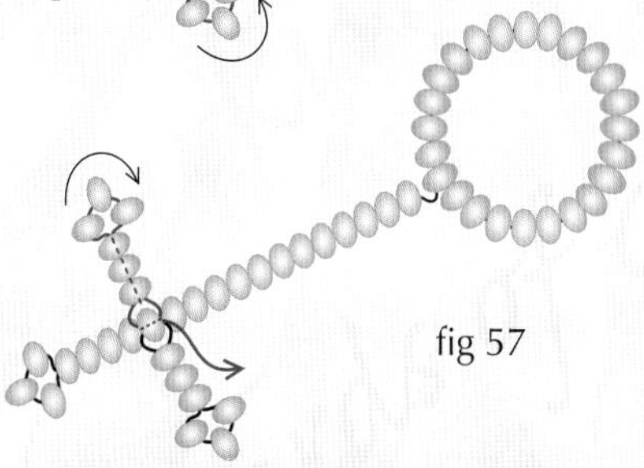

fig 57

Repeat Step 36 to make a second leaf rib on the opposite side of the main stem (fig 57).

37 Pass the needle through the following 3C along the main stem back towards the ring.

fig 58

Thread on 1C. Pass the needle through the previous 1C bead on the main stem in the same direction to bring the new bead parallel to this C bead (fig 58).

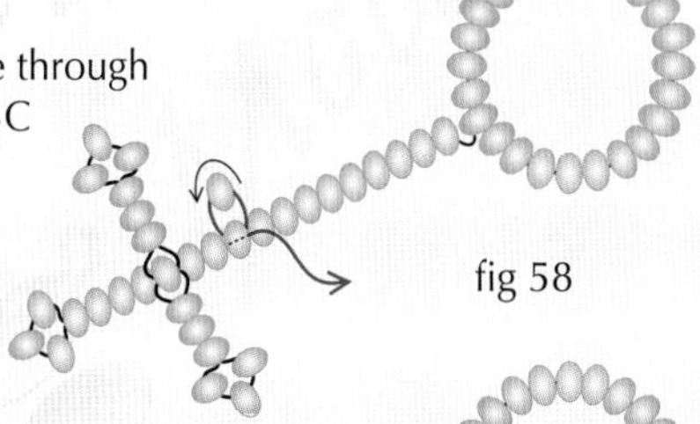

Pass the needle through the next 1C along the main stem and thread on 1C.

fig 59

Pass the needle through the previous 1C bead on the main stem in the same direction to bring the new bead parallel to this C (fig 59).

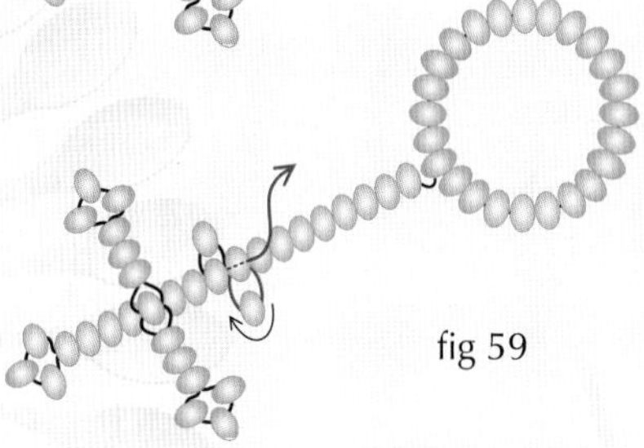

These two C single beads will support the inner curve of the holly leaf shape - their staggered positions help the leaf to twist and take on a more realistic holly-like profile.

Pass the needle through the following 3C along the main stem.

Repeat Step 36 to make two leaf ribs from this C bead on the main stem. Pass through the following 5C of the main stem.

38 Pass through the C bead on the ring in the same direction as before and back through the first 1C of the main leaf stem (fig 60).

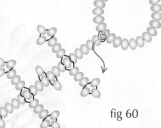

fig 60

fig 61

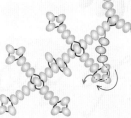

39 Thread on 3C. Pass through the 3C beads of the picot at the end of the closest leaf rib (fig 61).

Thread on 3C and pass through the closest single C bead attached to the middle of the main stem (fig 62).

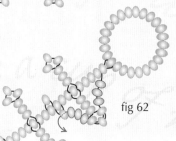

fig 62

Following fig 63 throughout -

Thread on 3C and pass through the 3C picot at the end of the next leaf rib along this edge of the leaf.

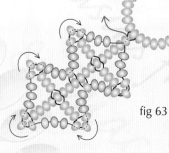

fig 63

Thread on 3C and pass through the 3C picot at the end of the main stem.
Thread on 3C and pass through the 3C picot at the end of the next leaf rib around.
Thread on 3C and pass through the single C bead on this side of the main stem.
Thread on 3C and pass through the 3C picot at the end of the final leaf rib.
Thread on 3C and pass through the first C bead of the main stem (fig 63). Pull the thread firmly.

41 Pass the needle through the following 4C beads around the ring (or the correct bead count for your ring) to be in the correct position the make the next leaf.

Repeat Steps 35 to 41 four times.
Repeat Steps 35 to 40 once to complete the sixth leaf.

42 The Berries - Pass the needle through the following 2C around the ring (or the appropriate number of C beads for your bead count) to emerge just past the centre of the plain ring section between the first two leaves.

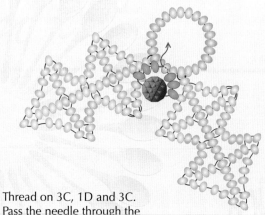

40 Pass the needle through the C bead on the ring, back up the main stem of the leaf, through the 3C picot at the end, back down the main stem and through the C bead on the ring.
Pull firmly (fig 64).

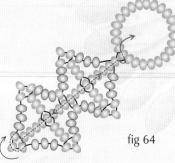

fig 64

The leaf will have crinkled into a single curve or an undulating curve - either profile is good and a mixture of both on the finished bauble is ideal.

Thread on 3C, 1D and 3C. Pass the needle through the previous C bead on the ring (fig 65).

fig 65

Place the ring on the bauble. You will see that the metal cap of the bauble is quite visible and spoils the effect. To partly conceal the cap you will need to add a little sprig of C beads to nestle behind the berry and against the cap.

Remove the ring from the bauble so it is easier to stitch, but remember which side of the berry bead (the cap side) you need the sprig to form.

44 Thread on 6C, 1D and 1C.

Pass the needle back through the D bead to pull the single C into an anchor. Pass through the following 4C and thread on 2C.

Pass the needle through the C bead on the ring once more (fig 69).

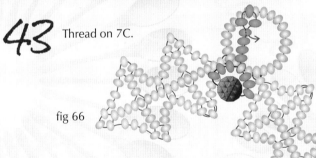

fig 69

Repeat Step 43 to add a set of C bead sprigs as before.

Pass the needle through the beads of the ring to emerge from the centre C bead between the next two leaves along.

Repeat Steps 42 to 44 twice more to add the remaining four berries and four sprigs to the ring.

Finish off the thread ends neatly and securely and place the ring over the bauble to sit on top of the brandy sauce swags.

45 The Hanging Loop - Prepare the needle with 1m of single emerald thread and tie a keeper bead 15cm from the end as before.

Thread on 1C, 1F, 1C and 1B. Pass the needle through the metal loop at the top of the bauble and back up through the four beads just added (fig 70).

Thread on 1B, 1C, 1E and 1C. Thread on 50C to make the loop.

Pass the needle back down the C bead above the E bead to pull up the beaded hanging loop.

Pass through the following 1E, 1C, 1B, 1C, 1F, 1C and 1B to emerge at the bauble loop.

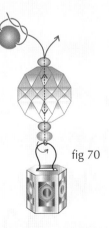

fig 70

Pass through the bauble loop and back up the beads to the base of the C bead loop.

Pass the needle through the C beads of the hanging loop and the beads of the connection to the bauble loop at least twice more to make the connection strong.

Finish off the thread ends neatly and securely.

43 Thread on 7C.

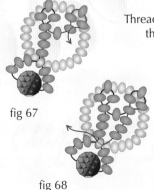

fig 66

Pass the needle back through the 4th C just added to make a 3C point as before (fig 66).

Thread on 5C. Pass the needle back through the 2nd C just added to make a second point (fig 67).

fig 67

Thread on 3C and pass through the C bead on the ring that supports the berry bead - make sure the needle is pointing in the same direction as before (fig 68).

fig 68

Pass the needle through the beads of the ring to emerge from the centre C bead between the next two leaves ready to add the next berry.

Prague Bauble

✷ ✷ ✷

You Will Need

Materials

One 40mm frosted teal glass bauble
11g of size 10/0 silver lined teal seed beads A
8g of frost metallic gold Twin beads B
3g of size 10/0 frost metallic gold seed beads C
3g of size 8/0 frost metallic gold seed beads D
Twenty-five 4mm teal fire polished faceted beads E
Thirteen 6mm teal fire polished faceted beads F
Turquoise size D beading thread

Tools

A size 10 beading needle
A pair of scissors to trim the threads

The opulence and grandeur of the Kingdom of Bohemia is reflected in the baroque sunburst motifs and elegant swags around the Prague Bauble. Try frosted silver Twin beads with black or lilac for a more contemporary look.

The Decoration is Made in Six Stages

A foundation row to fit around the neck of the bauble is made first.

A row of short loops is added to the foundation row.

The six long dangling strands are added next.

The large sunburst motifs are added to the strands around the middle of the bauble.

The swags between the strands complete the decoration over the bauble itself.

The hanging loop is added to the top of the bauble.

This design uses Twin beads - if you have not used them before see the technique notes on page 9.

1 The Foundation Row - **Prepare the needle with 1.5m of single thread and tie a keeper bead 15cm from the end.**

2 Thread on six repeats of 1B and 3A. Pass the needle through the same hole in the first B bead to make a ring (fig 1).

fig 1

fig 2

Place the ring over the neck of the bauble - it must fit snugly so you may need to adjust the bead count.

If you need to make an adjustment, add or subtract A beads equally from all six sections to keep the B beads evenly spaced around the ring.

Pass the needle through the beads of the ring once more to make it firm. Finish with the needle emerging from the first B bead (as fig 2).

3 Pass the needle through the outer hole of the first B bead to move to the outer edge of the ring (fig 3).

fig 3

Remove the ring from the bauble.

4 The Short Loops - Thread on 1A, 1C, 1A, 1B, 1A, 1C and 1A. Pass the needle through the outer hole of the next B bead around the ring (fig 4).

Repeat five more times to complete six small loops.

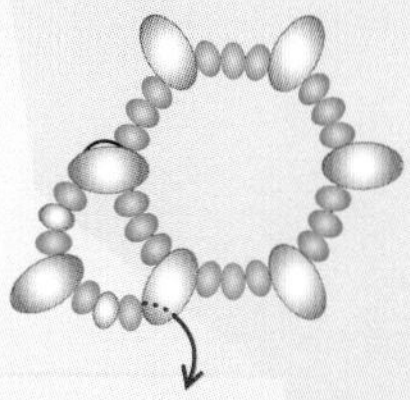

fig 4

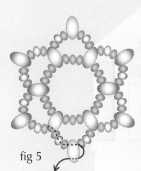

fig 5

Pass the needle through the following 1A, 1C, 1A and 1B of the first loop just made.

Pass through the outer hole of this B bead to be in the correct position for the next stage (fig 5).

5 The Long Strands - Thread on 7A, 1C, 1A, 1B, 1A, 1C, 10A, 1B, 1E, 1D, 10A, 1C, 1A, 1D, 1E, 1D, 2A, 1C, 3A and 1B.

Pass the needle through the second hole in the bottom B bead (fig 6). This bead is the first B of the small sun motif on the long strand.

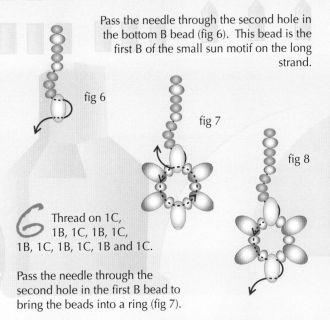

fig 6

fig 7

fig 8

6 Thread on 1C, 1B, 1C, 1B, 1C, 1B, 1C, 1B, 1C, 1B and 1C.

Pass the needle through the second hole in the first B bead to bring the beads into a ring (fig 7).

Referring to fig 8 pass the needle through the following 1C, 1B, 1C, 1B, 1C and 1B around the inside of the ring.

Pass through the outer hole of this B bead (fig 8).

7 Thread on 3A, 1D, 1A, 1F, 1C and 3A.

Leaving aside the last 3A to anchor the strand, pass the needle back up the last 1C and the following 1F, 1A and 1D (fig 9).

Referring to fig 10 thread on 3A and pass the needle through the outer hole of the B bead on the ring in the same direction to centralise the new sequence below this bead.

Pass the needle through the inner hole on this B bead (fig 10).

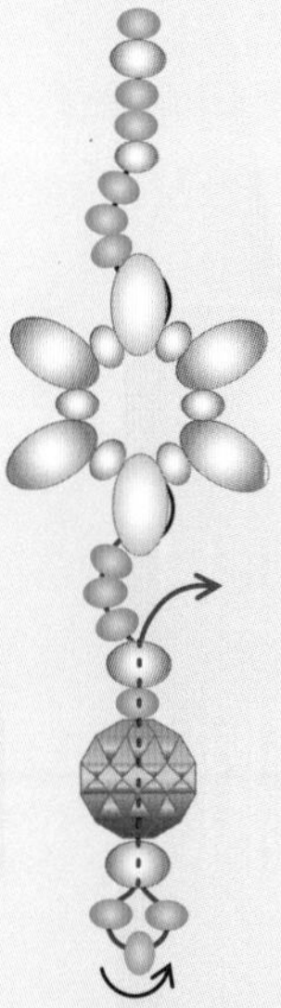

fig 10

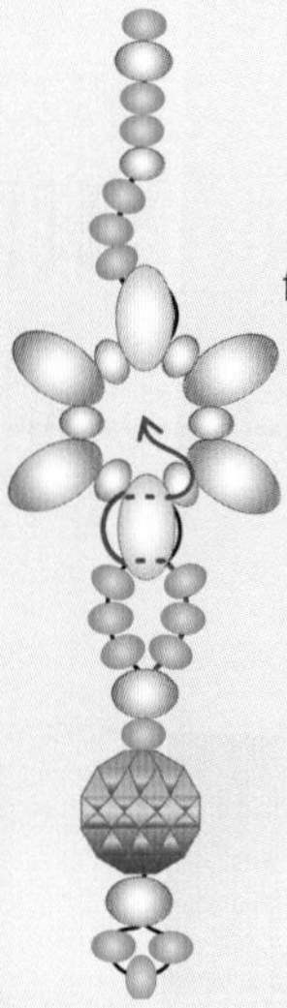

fig 9

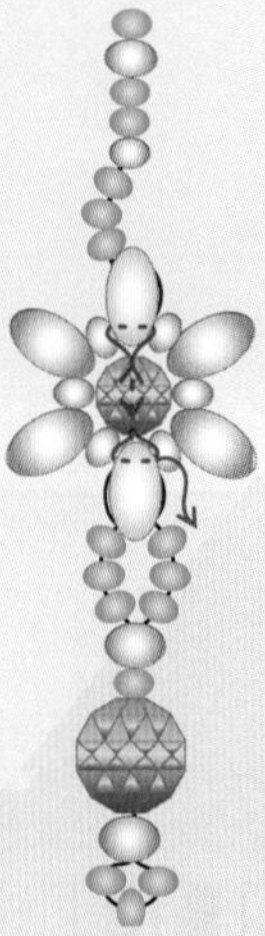

8 Thread on 1E.

Referring to fig 11 pass the needle through the inner hole of the first B of the ring, back through the E bead and through the B bead at the bottom of the ring.

This pulls the E bead into the centre of the ring and the thread into a figure of eight (fig 11).

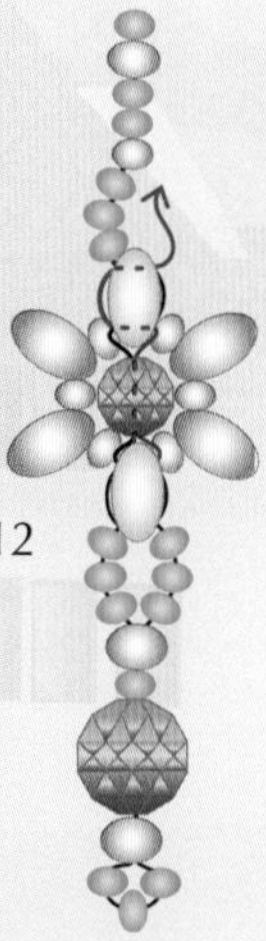

fig 11

9 Referring to fig 12 pass the needle back up the E bead and through the inner hole of the top B bead to emerge on the same side of this bead as the end of the long strand from the foundation ring.

Pass through the outer hole on this B bead (fig 12).

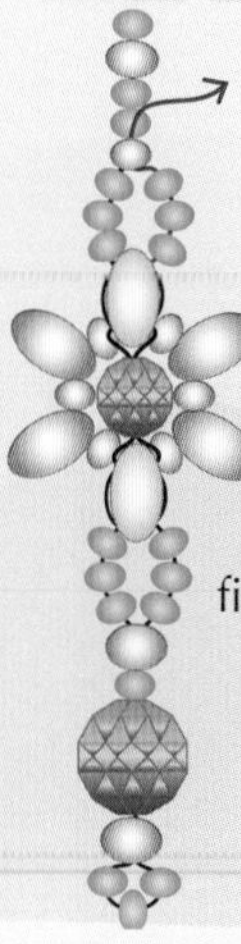

fig 12

fig 13

10 Thread on 3A.
Pass the needle up the last C bead of the long strand so the new motif hangs centrally on the end of the long strand (fig 13).

11 Pass the needle up through the following 2A, 1D, 1E, 1D, 1A, 1C, 10A, 1D and 1E beads to emerge just below the B bead.

Referring to fig 14 pass the needle up through the other hole in the B bead to centralise the E bead below it.

Thread on 10A, 1C, 1A, 1B, 1A, 1C and 7A.

Pass the needle through the B bead on the small loop at the top of the long strand (fig 14).

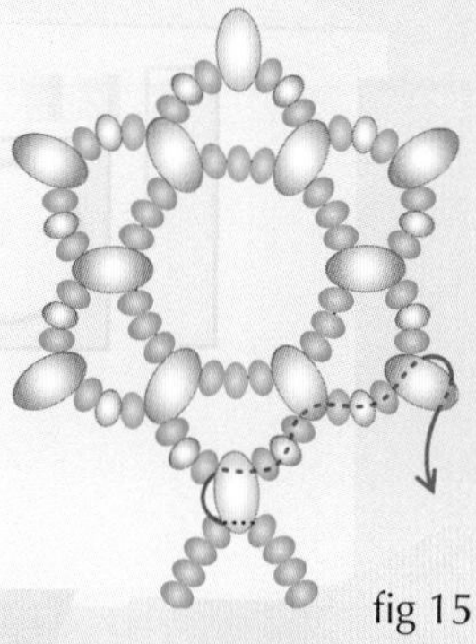

fig 14

12 Referring to fig 15 pass the needle through the other hole in this B bead and through the following 1A, 1C, 1A and 1B. Pass through the 1A, 1C, 1A and 1B of the next small loop along.

fig 15

Pass through the outer hole of this B bead.
This is the correct position to start the second long strand.

Repeat from Step 5 five times, to make six long strands in total, repositioning the needle each time for the next strand as in Step 12. Finish with the needle passing through the B bead at the top of the last long strand.

The long strands will now be linked together with the large sunburst motifs.

13 Following fig 16 pass the needle through the 1A, 1C and 1A of this small loop, the following 1B and the 1A, 1C, 1A and 1B of the next small loop.

Pass through the other hole of this B bead and down the first 7A, 1C, 1A and 1B of the attached long strand.

Pass up through the other hole of this B bead (fig 16).

This B bead and the adjacent B bead from the previous strand are now linked together to make the sunburst motif.

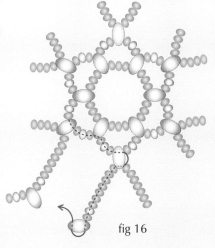

fig 16

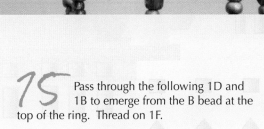 at right — photograph of finished beaded bauble.

Extra Info....
The sunburst motifs DO NOT sit between the two B beads at either side of an individual long strand but between one long strand and the next long strand around the bauble. Make sure your link matches fig 17.

14 The Sunburst Motifs -
Thread on 1D, 1B and 1D.

fig 17

Pass the needle down through the outer hole of the adjacent B bead on the previous strand (fig 17).

Make sure this strand is not twisted at the top so you are passing through the B bead on the correct side of the long strand.

Thread on 1D, 1B, 1D, 1B, 1D, 1B and 1D. Pass up through the first B bead to complete the ring (fig 18).

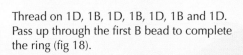

fig 18

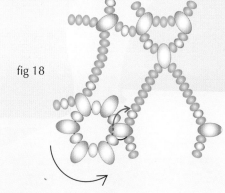

Pass the needle through the beads of the ring again to make it more firm.

15 Pass through the following 1D and 1B to emerge from the B bead at the top of the ring. Thread on 1F.

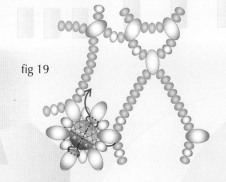

fig 19

Referring to fig 19 pass through the inner hole of the fourth B bead around the ring, back through the F bead and the B bead at the top of the ring to pull the F bead into the middle of the ring.

Extra Info....
The F bead may sit a little proud of the ring rather than in the central space - this is fine as it makes for a bolder motif when it sits against the bauble. However you must make sure that all of the sunburst motifs have the F beads sitting on the outer face of the rings.

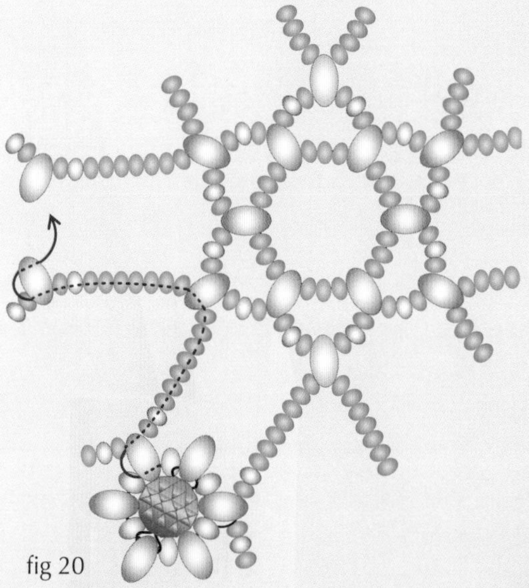

16
Referring to fig 20 pass the needle through the following 1D and 1B of the ring.

Pass the needle up through the other hole on this B bead and the following 1A, 1C and 7A of the previous long strand, the B bead at the top and down the 7A, 1C, 1A and 1B.

Pass up through the other hole of this B bead to be in the correct position to start the next sunburst motif (fig 20).

Repeat from Step 14 five more times to create six motifs in total. Finish with the needle emerging from the B bead at the top of the first long strand.

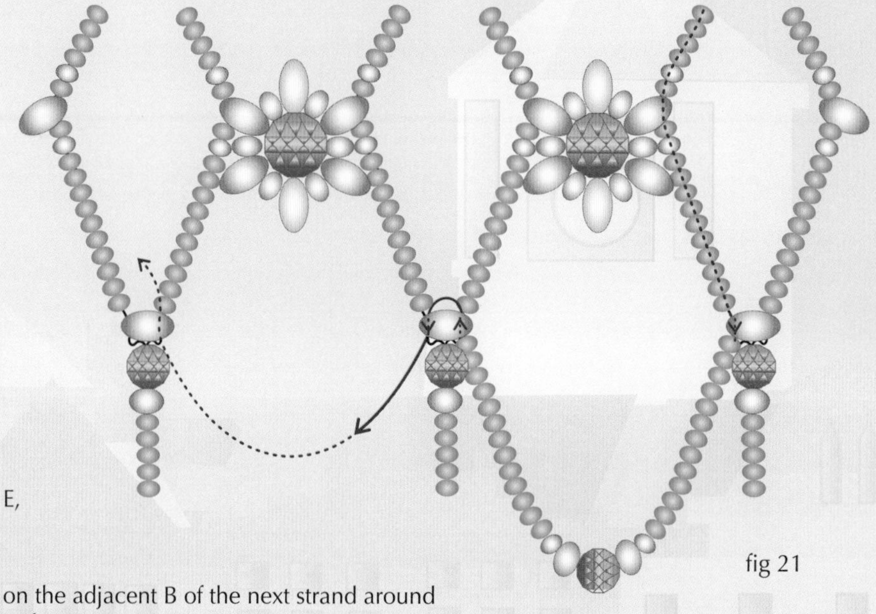

fig 20

17
The Swags - Pass the needle down through the first 7A, 1C, 1A, 1B, 1A, 1C, 10A and 1B of the long strand (see fig 21).

This B bead and the corresponding B beads around the decoration are linked together with a series of six simple swags.

Referring to fig 21 thread on 13A, 1C, 1D, 1E, 1D, 1C and 13A.

Pass the needle up through the nearest hole on the adjacent B of the next strand around and down through the other hole in this B bead.

Repeat until you have completed six swags.
Finish off the thread ends neatly and securely. Place the beadwork over the bauble.

fig 21

18 The Hanging Loop -
Prepare the needle with 1.2m of single thread and tie a keeper bead 15cm from the end.

Thread on six repeats of 1B and 1C.

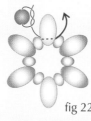

fig 22

Pass the needle through the same hole on the first B bead again to make a ring (fig 22).

Pass the needle through the beads of the ring again to make it firm.

fig 23

Thread on 1E and add to the centre of the ring as in Step 8 (fig 23).

50A
in total

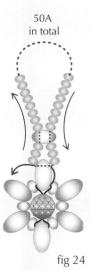

fig 24

19
Pass through the outer hole of the current B bead and thread on 3A, 1B and 50A.

Pass the needle down the other hole of the B bead to draw up the loop and thread on 3A.

Pass the needle through the B bead on the ring (fig 24).

Pass the needle through the beads just added twice more to strengthen the loop.

20
Pass the needle down through the B bead of the ring, the E bead and the opposite B bead to emerge from the outer hole of this B bead (fig 25).

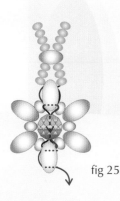

fig 25

21
Thread on 2A, 1D and 1F.

Pass the needle through the loop at the top of the bauble and back up through the 1F and 1D beads.

Thread on 2A and pass the needle through the B bead of the ring again (fig 26). Pass the needle through these new beads twice more to make the connection strong.

Finish off this and all remaining thread ends neatly and securely.

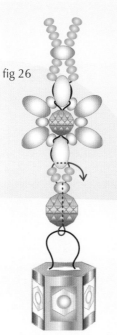

fig 26

Celestial Bauble

You Will Need

Materials

One 60mm gold frosted glass bauble
16g of pearl white Twin beads A
9g of size 10/0 pearl white seed beads B
10g of size 10/0 silver lined gold seed beads C
Four 8mm crystal AB fire polished faceted beads D
Four 6mm crystal AB fire polished faceted beads E
Thirty-three 4mm crystal AB fire polished
faceted beads F
Three 5mm gold filigree bead caps G
Golden yellow size D beading thread

Tools

A size 10 beading needle
A pair of scissors to trim the threads

A heavenly host and a scattering of stars bring a joyous Christmas message. The angel wings are stitched in pure white to stand out against the gold bauble, but place this same beading over a frosted silver bauble and the effect is made more subtle and delicate.

The Decoration is Made in Five Stages

The three angels are made first, adding the fringe strands to the lower body of each motif.

The three hanging star motifs are made next.

A foundation row is fitted around the neck of the bauble.

The angels and hanging stars are linked to the foundation row with swags of beads and more stars.

The hanging loop with a large star embellishment completes the decoration.

This design uses Twin beads - if you have not used them before see the technique notes on page 9.

1 The Angels - Prepare the needle with 1.2m of single thread and tie a keeper bead 15cm from the end.

2 Each wing starts with the top row - the following rows are worked backwards and forwards, from the tip of the wing to the body, to build up a curved profile.

Thread on 1D, 2B, 1A, 1B, 1A, 1B, 1A, 1B, 1A, 1B, 1A, 1B and 1A.

Pass the needle through the lower hole on the last A bead to bring a strap of thread down the side of the bead and reverse the direction of the needle (fig 1).

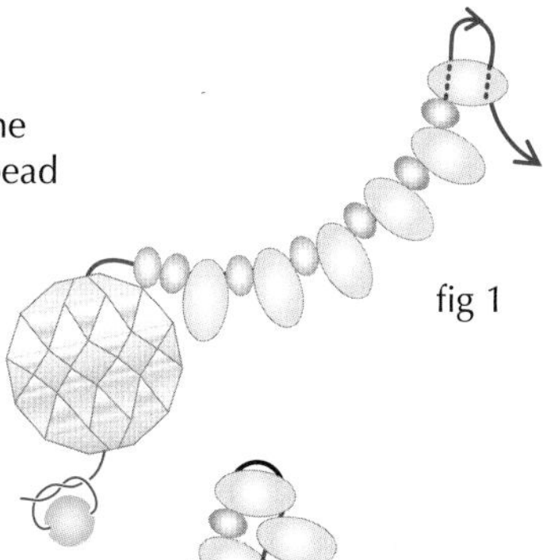

fig 1

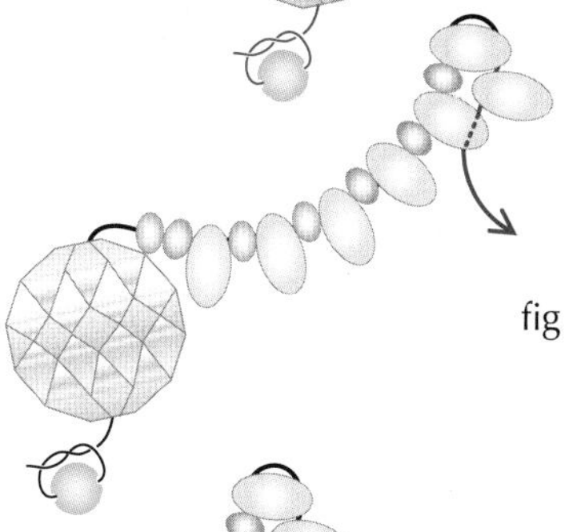

fig 2

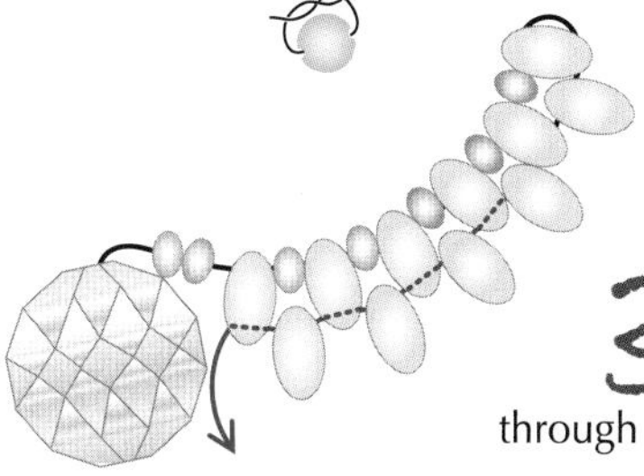

3 Thread on 1A and pass the needle through the free hole on the next A bead (fig 2).

Repeat to the end of the row to add 5A in total (fig 3).

fig 3

4 Thread on 1A and pass the needle through the lower hole on the last A bead of the previous row to start the new row (fig 4).

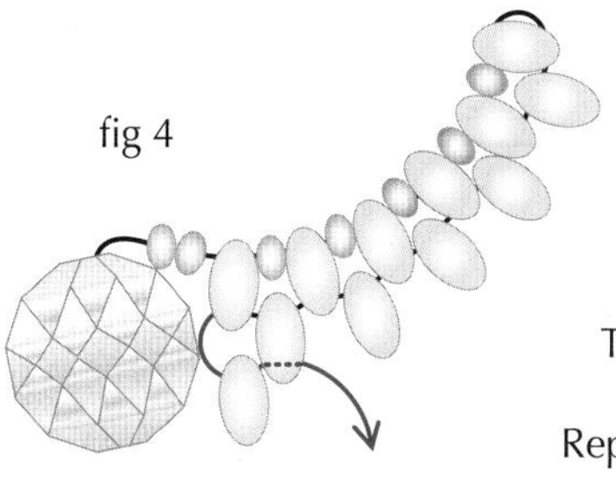

fig 4

Make two more 1A stitches as on the previous row.

Thread on 1B and 1A for the fourth stitch. Repeat for the fifth stitch of the row (fig 5).

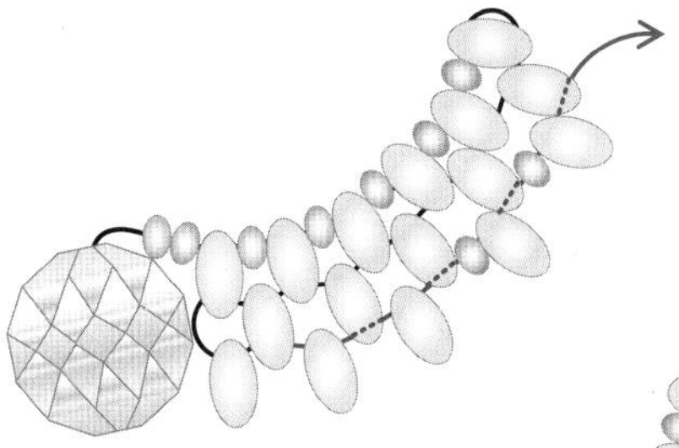

fig 5

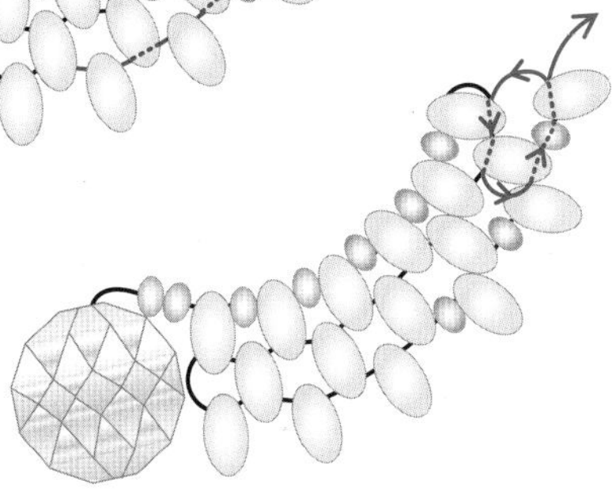

fig 6

5 Thread on 1B and 1A.
Referring to fig 6 pass through the lower hole of the last A on the first row and the top hole on the first A of the second row. Pass back through the lower hole on this A bead, the last B bead added and the top hole on the following A bead (fig 6).

The needle will be emerging from the top hole of the last A bead added to the work.

9 Thread on 1A. Pass the needle through the lower hole in the previous A bead and the same hole in the new A to make a Square stitch (fig 9) - the needle should be pointing back along the previous row.

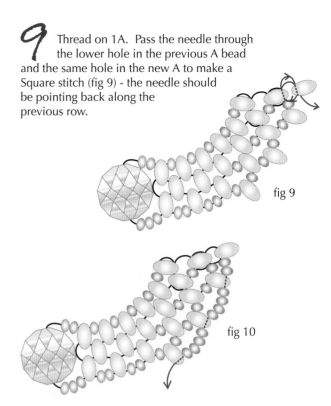

fig 9

fig 10

6 Pass the needle through the lower hole on the current A bead to change the direction of the needle and start the new row.

Thread on 1B, 1A and 1B. Pass though the lower hole on the next A bead along. Repeat this stitch twice. Make the next two stitches with 2B beads only (fig 7).

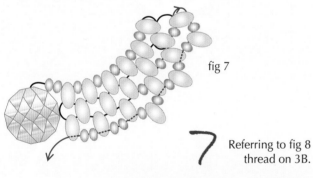

fig 7

7 Referring to fig 8 thread on 3B.

Pass the needle through the D bead to emerge at the top edge of the wing. Pass the needle through the holes in the B and A beads along the top edge of the wing.

8 Pass through the lower hole on the end A bead and the top hole of the following A. Pass through the lower hole of this A and the following 1B.

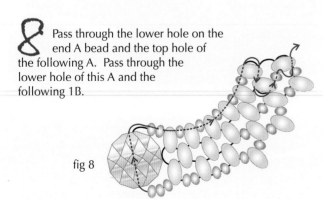

fig 8

Pass the needle through the lower hole of the next A to emerge from the lowest A bead hole at the end of the wing (fig 8).

10 Thread on 2B and pass through the lower hole in the first A bead back along the lower edge of the wing. Add 4B beads into each of the next two spaces (fig 10).

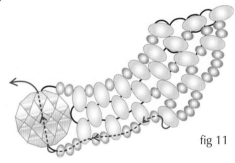

fig 11

Referring to fig 11 pass the needle through the following 1B, 1A, 2B, 1A, 2B, 1A and 3B of the lower wing edge and up through the D bead.

The needle is now in the correct position to start the second wing.

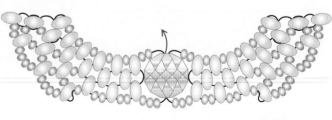

fig 12

Repeat from Step 2 to make a second wing on the other side of the D bead (fig 12).

11 The Head and Halo - Thread on 1B, 1E, 1B, 1G (from the outside of the cup to the inside) and 1C.

Leaving aside the 1C to anchor the strand pass the needle back through the middle hole of the G cap and the following beads to emerge at the bottom of the D bead (fig 13).

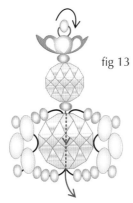

fig 13

12 The Fringed Skirt - You need to make seven fringe strands. One strand hangs from each of the 3B beads on either side of the needle position. The seventh strand will hang from an extra B bead that will be added in the central gap.

Pass the needle through 1B bead along the bottom edge of the wing and *thread on 27C, 3B, 1C, 5B, 1C, 1B, 1F, 1B and 3C.

Leaving aside the last 3C beads to anchor the strand pass the needle back up the bottom B bead (fig 14). Pass through the following beads to the top of the strand.

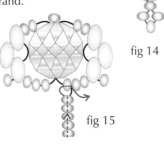

fig 14

fig 15

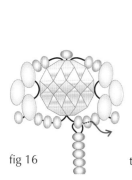

fig 16

Pass the needle through the same B bead on the wing edge in the same direction to centralise the strand (fig 15).

If necessary adjust the tension in the thread so the strand falls softly with a minimal amount of thread showing at the top.

Pass the needle through the next B bead along the lower edge of the wing (fig 16).

13 Thread on 23C, 3B, 1C, 5B, 1C, 1B, 1F, 1B and 3C. Make the anchor at the bottom as before, pass the needle to the top of the strand and through the B bead on the wing edge in the same direction. Adjust the thread tension if required.

Pass the needle through the third B bead along the wing ready to make the next tassel strand.

Thread on 19C, 3B, 1C, 5B, 1C, 1B, 1F, 1B and 3C. Make the strand as before, passing the needle through the B bead on the wing edge in the same direction and adjusting the thread tension if required.

The needle now has to be turned around to point in the opposite direction.

14 Pass through the following 1A, 2B and 1A along the lower wing edge.

Pass back through the other hole in this A bead to change the needle direction.

Pass through the 2B on the lower edge and the following 1A (fig 17).

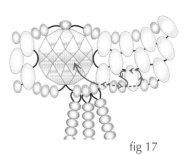

fig 17

fig 18

15 Pass the needle through the 3B beads supporting the fringe strands and thread on 1B.

Pass the needle through the first B bead on the lower edge of the opposite wing pulling the new B bead into the gap between the two wings (fig 18). The needle is now in the correct position to make the first fringe strand on this side of the angel.

Repeat from the * in Step 12 to the end of Step 14 to make three fringe strands and turn the needle as before.

Pass the needle through the 3B beads supporting the fringe strands just made and the following 1B added in step 15. This bead supports the central (longest) fringe strand.

16 Thread on 31C, 3B, 1C, 5B, 1C, 1B, 1F, 1B and 3C. Make the strand as before, passing the needle through the single B bead at the top in the same direction and adjusting the thread tension if required.

Pass the needle through the following 3B beads along the following wing edge to ensure the central B bead is well supported.

Finish off this thread end neatly and securely. Remove the keeper bead and secure this end in a similar fashion.

Make two more angels to match.

17 The Star Motifs - Prepare the needle as in Step 1 with 1.2m of single thread and tie a keeper bead 15cm from the end.

Thread on 6A. Pass the needle through the same hole in the first A bead again to make a tight circle of 6A (fig 19).

Pass the needle through the same holes of the 6A again to make the circle firm.

Pass the needle through the outer hole on the current A bead ready to add the star points.

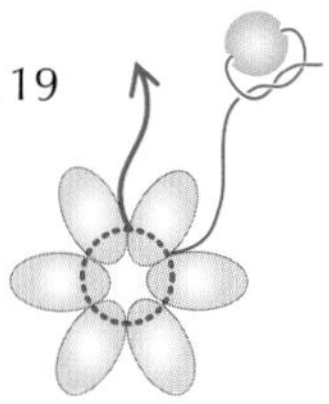

fig 19

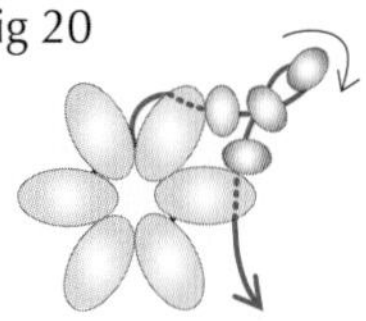

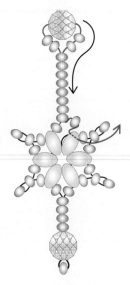

fig 20

18 Thread on 3C.

Leaving aside the last 1C bead to anchor the strand pass the needle back through the middle C bead.

Thread on 1C and pass the needle through the outer hole of the next A bead around the circle (fig 20) - make sure you pass through the hole in the correct direction to position the C bead point across the gap.

Repeat to make a second point in the next gap (see fig 21).

fig 21

19 In the next gap thread on 3C, 2B, 1F and 1B. Leaving aside the last B to anchor the strand pass the needle back up the F and the following 2B and 2C beads. Thread on 1C and pass the needle through the outer hole of the next A bead around the circle (fig 21).

Make two plain points in the next two gaps.

20 The sixth gap - Thread on 3C, 6B, 2C, 1F and 2C.

Pass the needle back through the following 6B and 2C to make a long spur.

Thread on 1C and pass though the outer hole of the next A bead around the circle to close up the star motif (fig 22).

Finish off both thread ends neatly and securely. Repeat to make two more star motifs to match.

fig 22

21 The Foundation Row - Prepare the needle with 1.2m of single thread and tie a keeper bead 15cm from the end.

Thread on three repeats of 1F, 1B, 2C, 1A, 2C and 1B.

Pass the needle through the first F bead to draw the beads into a ring (fig 23).

Place the ring over the neck of the bauble - it needs to fit snugly so you may need to adjust the bead count.

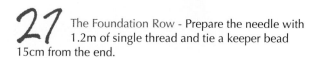

fig 23

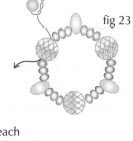

If you need to make an adjustment rethread the ring changing the C bead count in each gap. You need the A and F beads evenly spaced around the neck of the bauble.

fig 24

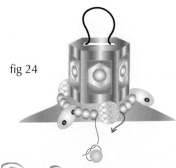

Pass the needle through the beads of the ring once more to make it firm. Finish with the needle emerging from an F bead (fig 24).

Remove the ring from the bauble.

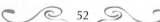

22
Linking the Motifs - Thread on 1B, 4C, 1B, 1F, 1B and 14C. Pass the needle through the C bead inside the halo of the first angel.

Pass the needle back through the 14C, 1B, 1F and 1B beads just added.

Thread on 4C and 1B and pass the needle through the F bead on the foundation ring in the same direction (fig 25).

Pass the needle through the following beads of the ring to emerge from the next F bead around.

Repeat to add the second angel.
Repeat once more to attach the third angel to the third F bead of the foundation ring.

Pass the needle through the beads of the foundation ring to emerge from the next A bead along.

fig 25

23
Pass the needle through the lower hole in this A bead and thread on 2B, 3C and 1A. Pass the needle through the lower hole on this A bead (fig 26).

fig 26

24
Thread on 5A and pass the needle through the lower hole of the A bead added in Step 23 to make a circle (fig 27). Pass the needle through these holes again to make the circle firm.

Locate the first A bead added in Step 23 and if necessary pass the needle around the circle so the needle is emerging from the lower (inner) hole of this A bead (as fig 27).

Pass through the outer hole on this A bead to point away from the 2B, 3C and 1A beads (fig 28).

fig 27

fig 28

25
Thread on 3C. Leave aside the last C bead and pass back through the second C. Thread on 1C and pass through the outer hole in the next A bead around the circle as before (fig 29).

Repeat this stitch in the next gap to make a second star point.

fig 29

26
Referring to fig 30 throughout, thread on 3C, 6B and 1C.

Lay the work out flat in front of you.

Pass the needle down through the free hole of the A bead on the tip of the angel wing on the left.

Thread on 2C.

Pass the needle through the F bead at the top of the spur on the first star motif made in Steps 17 to 20.

Thread on 2C and pass up through the outer hole on the tip of the angel wing on the right.

Thread on 1C and 6B. Locate the lowest C beads threaded into the current gap on the new star motif and pass the needle up through these 2C beads.

Thread on 1C and pass the needle through the outer hole on the next A bead around the A bead circle (fig 30).

fig 30

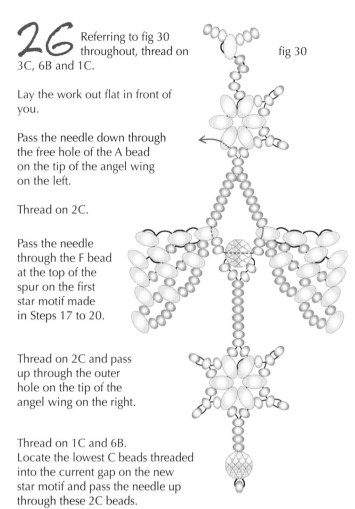

27 Make two plain points in the next two gaps around the A bead circle as before - the needle should emerge from the outer hole in the sixth A bead.

Thread on 1C and pass the needle up through the middle 1C of the 3C in this gap. Pass through the following 1C and thread on 2B.

Pass through the hole in the A bead on the foundation ring in the same direction as before (fig 31).

fig 31

Pass the needle through the other hole in this A bead and the following beads of the foundation ring to emerge from the next A bead around.

Repeat from Step 23 twice to add the star motifs and complete the links in the remaining two gaps.

Finish off all of the remaining thread ends neatly and securely. Place the beading over the bauble.

28 The Hanging Loop - Prepare the needle with 1.2m of single thread and tie a keeper bead 15cm from the end. As in fig 19 make a circle of 6A beads, make it firm with a second pass of the needle and pass the needle through the outer hole of the first A bead.

Thread on 1A and pass through the next outer hole around.

Repeat to add 6A in total (fig 32). Pass the needle through these beads again to make this larger circle firm.

fig 32

Pass the needle through the outer hole of the current A bead ready to add the star points (see fig 33).

29 Thread on 5C. Pass the needle back through the fourth C bead and thread on 3C. Pass the needle through the outer hole of the next A bead around (fig 33).

fig 33

Repeat twice more to complete three points.

The current A bead is now used as a support for the hanging loop.

50C in total

fig 34

30 Thread on 2C, 1B, 1E, 1B and 50C.

Pass the needle back down the top B bead and the following 1E and 1B to draw up the loop.

Thread on 2C and pass through the outer hole of the A bead in the same direction (fig 34).

Pass the needle up through the connection beads, around the loop and back down to pass through the A bead twice more to make the loop as strong as possible.

31 Make a star point in the next three gaps around the A bead circle to complete six points in total. The needle should be emerging from the A bead opposite the hanging loop - this is where you need to connect to the bauble.

Thread on 2C, 1B, 1D and 1B. Pass the needle through the loop at the top of the bauble and back up through the 1B, 1D and 1B beads.

fig 35

Thread on 2C and pass the needle through the A bead on the circle in the same direction (fig 35).

Pass the needle down and back up through this connection at least twice more to make it strong.

Finish off this and any remaining thread ends neatly and securely.

Snowflake Strands

Matching the pearly white Twin beads with pearly white seed beads transforms the six-pointed star motif into a snowflake. String three different sizes together and you have a delicate wisp of ice to twinkle on the tree.

32 The Large Snowflake - Work Step 28.
*Thread on 3B, 1F and 1B. Pass the needle back through the F bead and thread on 3B. Pass through the outer hole of the next A bead around (fig 36). Repeat from * once.

fig 36

25B total

fig 37

Adding the Top Loop - Thread on 3B, 1F, 1B, 1H, 1D, 1H and 25B. Pass the needle back down the 1H, 1D, 1H, 1B and 1F beads. Thread on 3B and pass through the outer hole of the next A bead around (fig 37).

Add three more points as before to complete the snowflake. Pass the needle through all the beads added in Step 32 once more and remove the needle.

33 The Medium Snowflake - Work Step 28.

Thread on 4B. Pass the needle back through the third B bead and thread on 2B. Pass the needle through the outer hole of the next A bead. Repeat once.

Link to the Large Snowflake - Thread on 4B, 1H, 1E and 1H. Pass the needle through the B bead at the tip of the large snowflake point opposite the top loop. Pass back through the last H bead and the following 1E, 1H and 2B. Thread on 2B and complete the point as before (fig 38).

fig 38

Add three more 4B points to complete the snowflake and remove the needle.

34 The Small Snowflake - Work Steps 17 and 18 using A and B beads only.

Referring to Step 19 start the next (bottom) point with 3B, 1H, 1E, 1H, 1B, 1H, 1F, 1H and 1B. Pass the needle back up through the last H bead and the following eight beads completing the point with 1B as in fig 21.

Make two 3B points in the next two gaps. For the last gap repeat the link in Step 33 starting with 3B rather than 4B to attach this snowflake to the bottom of the medium snowflake.

Finish off all thread ends neatly and securely.

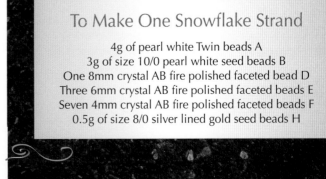

You Will Need

To Make One Snowflake Strand

4g of pearl white Twin beads A
3g of size 10/0 pearl white seed beads B
One 8mm crystal AB fire polished faceted bead D
Three 6mm crystal AB fire polished faceted beads E
Seven 4mm crystal AB fire polished faceted beads F
0.5g of size 8/0 silver lined gold seed beads H

Monarch Bauble

You Will Need

Materials

One 60mm frosted red glass bauble
6g of size 10/0 transparent purple AB seed beads A
5g of size 10/0 silver lined gold seed beads B
3g of size 8/0 silver lined red seed beads C
2g of size 8/0 chalk black seed beads D
10g of size 10/0 transparent frost red seed beads E
3g of size 6/0 transparent purple AB seed beads F
Fourteen 4mm red fire polished faceted beads G
Seventeen 6mm red fire polished faceted beads H
Seven 4mm black fire polished faceted beads J
Seven 7x5mm black fire polished faceted drops K
Seven 6mm purple AB fire polished faceted beads L
One 12mm red fire polished faceted bead M
Red size D beading thread

Tools

A size 10 beading needle
A pair of scissors to trim the threads

*J*ewel-like butterflies flutter around this decoration. Pick out the wings in crystal AB, gold and pearl white for a sophisticated combination on a frosted silver bauble, or extend the fringe strands with crystal beads for true opulence.

The Decoration is Made in Five Stages

The six fringed butterflies are made first.

A foundation row around the neck of the bauble is created next.

The butterflies are linked to the foundation row with swags of beads.

A small decorative motif is added to the swags allowing them to be adjusted for a good fit.

The hanging loop with butterfly embellishment completes the decoration.

1 The Butterflies - Prepare the needle with 1.2m of single thread and tie a keeper bead 15cm from the end.

Thread on 2D. Pass the needle back through the first D to bring the other bead to sit at 90° across the hole (fig 1).

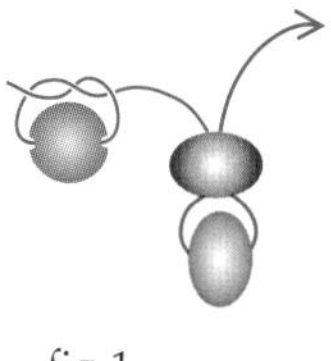

fig 1

2 Thread on 1K (narrow end first) and 1J.
Pass the needle back down the K bead to emerge alongside the keeper bead (fig 2). Make sure the J bead sits at 90° to the end of the drop bead as in fig 2.

Remove the keeper bead and tie the two thread ends together, pulling the knots between the beads to secure the work.

fig 2

fig 3

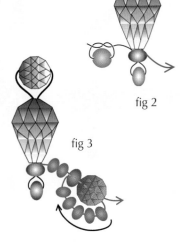

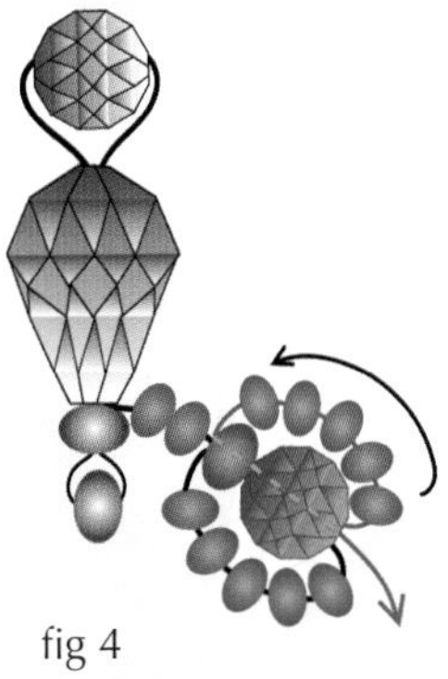

fig 4

3 Thread on 2A, 1C, 1G and 5A.

Pass the needle through the 1C and 1G bead again to bring the 5A beads into a strap along the side of the C and G beads (fig 3).

Thread on 5A and pass through the C and G beads again to make a second strap (fig 4).

fig 5

4 Pass the needle through the 5A beads of the first strap and the 2A beads below the C bead (fig 5).

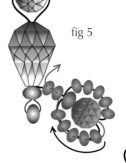

fig 6

5 Thread on 3A, 1C, 1H, 3B and 5A. Pass the needle through the C and H beads to make a strap on the side as before (fig 6).

Thread on 3B and 5A. Pass the needle through the C and H beads to make a second strap.

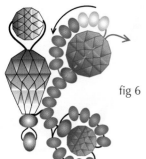

fig 7

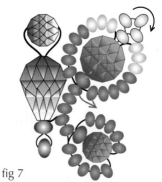

6 Thread on 4B.
Pass the needle back through the first 1B of the 4B just added, the H bead and the following 1C to leave a 3B picot at the top (fig 7).

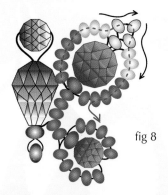

7 Pass the needle through the 5A and 3B of the first strap.

Pass the needle through the 3B beads of the picot and the following 3B and 4A of the second strap (fig 8).

Read the Extra Info below.

fig 8

10 Thread on 1A and pass the needle down through the K bead of the body to draw the wing into place (fig 12).

The needle is now in the correct position to make the second wing.

Repeat from the start of Step 3 to make a second wing.

fig 12

Extra Info....

When the thread follows a single path through a connection between two larger elements the work can flip backwards and forwards. Look at the A beads framing the G bead made in Step 3.

Along one side of the G bead the A beads are now continuous with the line of A beads up the side of the K bead.

On the other side of the G bead the 5A bead strap connects to the G bead and C bead only. If necessary, flip the G bead over to bring this 5A strap alongside the current needle position as in fig 8.

11 Having completed the second wing the needle should be emerging between the K bead and the first D bead. The connection of both wings to the body and to the head bead need to be strengthened before you move on to the fringing.

Following fig 13, pass the needle through the 5A beads up the side of the K bead, through the single A bead that connects to the top of the K bead and through the hole in the J bead.

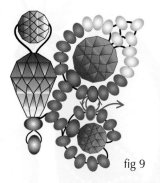

8 Referring to fig 9, pass the needle through the fourth A bead of the 5A strap towards the outer end of the G bead.

Pass through the A bead on the H bead frame and through the A bead on the G bead frame once more to make a Square stitch (fig 9).

fig 9

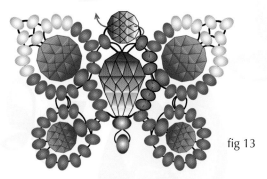

fig 13

Referring to fig 14, pass the needle through the single A bead at the top of the other wing and down through the following 7A beads along this side of the K bead to emerge adjacent to the lower C bead.

9 Pass the needle through the following 3A beads of the G bead frame and thread on 2A. Pass the needle through the following 1A on the other side of the G bead (fig 10).

Pass the needle through the following 4A of the frame, the 2A below the C bead and the 3A leading up to the other C bead.

fig 10

Pass through the first 2A of the A bead strap on the top edge of the H bead frame (fig 11).

fig 14

Pass the needle through the C bead, the G bead and the 2A beads added in Step 9 to point downwards from the lower edge of the wing (fig 14).

The first three fringe strands attach to this A bead and the following 2A along the edge.

fig 11

12

Thread on 5E, 1B, 1A, 1B, 1C, 1F and 1B.

Leaving aside the last 1B to anchor the strand pass the needle back up the F bead and the following nine beads just added.

Pass through the A bead on the wing edge in the same direction to complete the strand and centre it below the A bead on the wing (fig 15).

If necessary adjust the tension in the thread so the strand falls softly from the A bead of the wing edge.

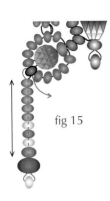

fig 15

13

Referring to fig 16, pass though the next A bead along the wing edge and thread on 9E, 1B, 1A, 1B, 1C, 1F and 1B for the next fringe strand. Make the strand as before, passing through the A bead on the wing edge to centralise the strand.

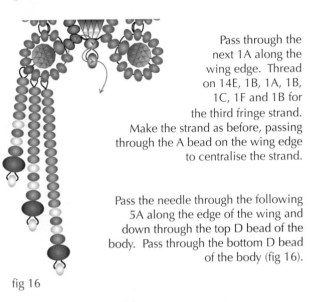

Pass through the next 1A along the wing edge. Thread on 14E, 1B, 1A, 1B, 1C, 1F and 1B for the third fringe strand. Make the strand as before, passing through the A bead on the wing edge to centralise the strand.

Pass the needle through the following 5A along the edge of the wing and down through the top D bead of the body. Pass through the bottom D bead of the body (fig 16).

fig 16

14

Thread on 22E, 1B, 1A, 1B, 1C, 1L, 1C and 3B.

Leaving aside the last 3B pass the needle up through the last C bead and the following 26 beads to emerge 1E bead from the top of the strand.

Thread on 1E and pass the needle through the D bead at the bottom of the body to centralise the strand.

Adjust the tension in the thread as before to make the strand hang softly (fig 17).

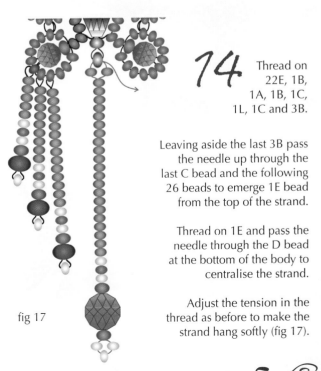

fig 17

15

Pass the needle up the following D bead, down through the first 2A of the other wing, the C bead and the following G bead.

Pass though the 2A added in Step 9 ready to start the fringe strands on this wing (fig 18).

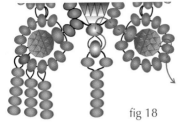

fig 18

Repeat from Step 12 to make three matching fringe strands on this wing. Leave the thread ends loose and set aside.

Repeat from Step 1 to make five more butterfly motifs to match.

16

The Foundation Row - Prepare the needle with 1.2m of single thread and tie a keeper bead 15cm from the end.

Thread on six repeats of 1A, 1D, 1A and 3E.

fig 19

Pass the needle through the first 1A, 1D and 1A to bring the beads into a ring (fig 19).

fig 20

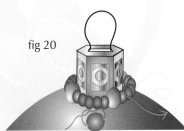

Place the ring over the neck of the bauble - it needs to fit snugly so you may need to adjust the bead count.

If you need to make an adjustment, change the E bead count on all six repeats until you have the six 1A, 1D, 1A sequences equally spaced around the bauble neck (fig 20).

Remove the ring from the bauble and pass the needle through all of the beads of the foundation row again to make it more firm.

Finish with the needle emerging from the second A bead of a 1A, 1D, 1A sequence (as fig 19).

17

Connecting the Butterflies to the Foundation Row - Thread on 20E.

Pick up the first butterfly motif and locate the 3B picot at the top of one of the wings.

Pass the needle through the middle B of the picot to emerge pointing away from the butterfly head and down the outer edge of the wing (see fig 21).

Referring to fig 21 pass the needle through the following 4B and 4A along the outer edge of this top wing.

fig 21

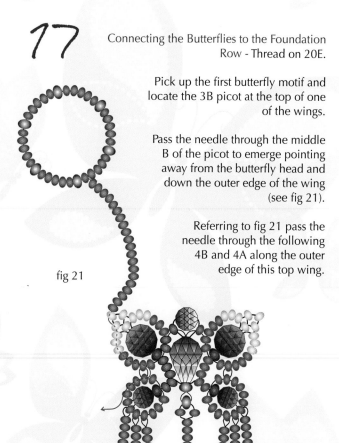

Pass the needle through the A bead of the lower wing that makes the link to the top wing and the following 3A (fig 21).

18

Thread on 10E. Pick up the next butterfly motif and locate the 3B picot at the top of the wing.

This time pass the needle through the middle B bead of the picot to emerge pointing towards the butterfly head and along the top edge of the wing (see fig 22).

fig 22

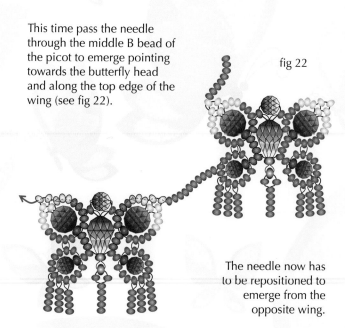

The needle now has to be repositioned to emerge from the opposite wing.

Referring to fig 22 pass the needle through the following 4B and 3A of the top edge of the wing, the 1A bead adjacent to the J bead and through the J bead. Pass through the following 4A and 5B along the top edge of the second wing to emerge pointing away from the butterfly head (fig 22).

19 Thread on 10E.

Pick up the next butterfly motif and find the second A bead along from the shortest fringe strand on the outer edge of the lower wing (see fig 23).

Pass the needle through this A bead and the following 3A to emerge between the wings on this side of the butterfly.

Pass the needle through the linked A bead on the upper wing and the following 3A and 3B. Pass the needle through the first 2B beads of the picot to emerge pointing towards the head of the butterfly (fig 23).

Thread on 20E.

Pass the needle through the 1A, 1D and 1A beads on the ring that support the previous 20E swag, in the same direction, to emerge alongside the top of that swag (fig 24).

This completes the first set of connections.

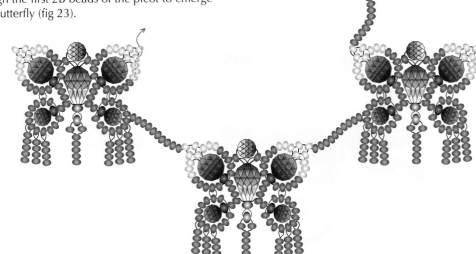

fig 23

fig 24

20 Pass the needle through the beads of the foundation row to emerge from the fourth A bead around (fig 25). This is the correct position to start the second set of connections.

Repeat Steps 17 and 18 to add a swag of 20E to connect up the fourth butterfly motif and a swag of 10E to add the fifth motif.

fig 25

21 Thread on 10E. This swag needs to be connected to the lower wing on the very first butterfly.

Lay the work out flat so you can check that the butterflies are lying flat and there are no twists in the existing connections (see fig 26).

As in fig 23 pass the needle up through the 2nd A bead above the shortest fringe strand. Pass up through the following beads of this edge of the motif to emerge from the middle bead of the top picot (fig 26).

Thread on 20E and complete the swag by passing through the 1A, 1D and 1A beads on the foundation row (see figs 24 and 27).

This completes the second set of connections.

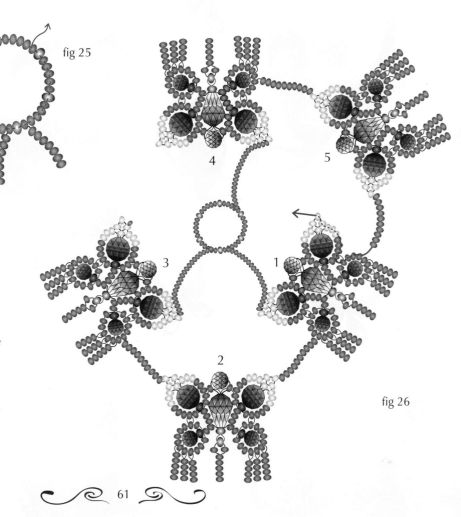

fig 26

22 The remaining (sixth) butterfly connects to both the third and the fourth butterflies already added to the foundation row (see fig 27 which shows the butterflies numbered in order of assembly).

Pass the needle through the beads of the foundation row to emerge from the 4th A bead around the ring to be in the correct start position.

Lay the work flat so you can see which butterfly you need to attach first (the third motif you added to the design).

Thread on 20E.

As in Step 17 locate the correct B bead on the picot at the tip of the top wing and pass down through the beads along the wing edges to emerge at the correct position to start the 10E swag (as fig 21).

Thread on 10E, connect to the sixth butterfly motif and reposition the needle as in Step 18 ready to make the last 10E swag.

Thread on 10E and locate the correct A bead for this link on the lower wing of the fourth motif.

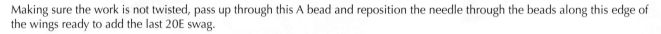

fig 27

Making sure the work is not twisted, pass up through this A bead and reposition the needle through the beads along this edge of the wings ready to add the last 20E swag.

Make the 20E swag as before connecting it to the foundation row through the correct 1A, 1D and 1A beads.

Place the beadwork over the bauble. The three higher butterflies will tend to fold forwards away from the bauble surface so the next stage is to tighten the swags.

23 Tightening the Swags - The needle should be emerging from the second A bead of a 1A, 1D and 1A sequence.

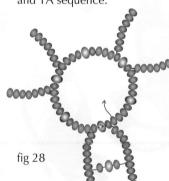

fig 28

Pass the needle down through the first 6E beads of the following swag. Thread on 1E, 1D and 1E.

Pass the needle up through the top 6E of the adjacent swag and the 1A, 1D and 1A beads on the foundation row (fig 28). Pull the thread firmly to close up the gaps.

Pass the needle through the foundation row to emerge from the 4th A bead around the bauble neck and repeat. Repeat once more to complete three 3-bead bridges between the swags.

Look again at how the swags and the butterflies sit against the bauble - the three higher butterflies should be lying more flat improving the spacing of the design. If your butterflies are still not lying satisfactorily remove the needle and unpick the 3-bead bridges.

Start Step 23 again passing the needle down through 7E or 8E beads of the first swag, adding the three bridge beads and up through the corresponding number of E beads on the adjacent swag. Repeat twice. This will cinch in the swags a little more and improve the lie of the butterflies.

24

Making the Small Motif - Pass the needle through the beads of the first swag to emerge from the D bead at the middle of the first 3-bead bridge.

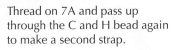

Thread on 3D and pass the needle through the D on the bridge to make a small ring. Pass through the first 2D just added (fig 29).

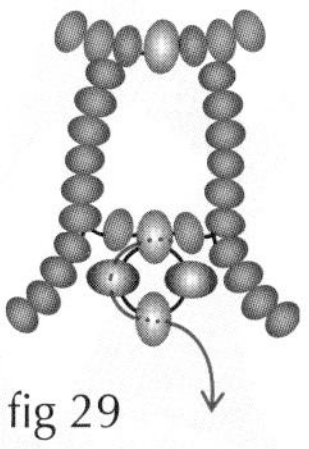

fig 29

Thread on 1H, 1C and 3A. Pass the needle back through the C and H beads to pull the 3A into a picot.

Pass the needle through the lowest D bead of the ring in the same direction to centre the new beads (fig 30).

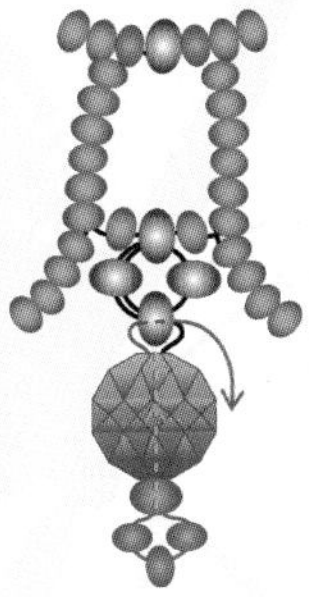

fig 30

Thread on 7A. Pass the needle through the C and H beads to make a strap on the side of the motif. Pass through the D bead on the ring in the opposite direction (fig 31).

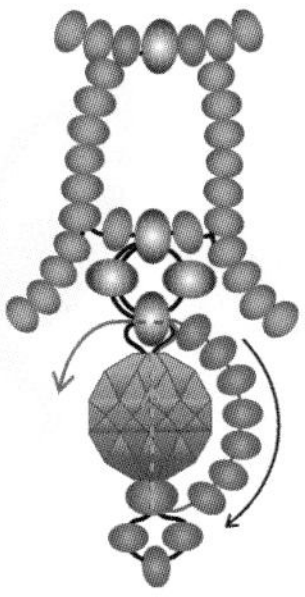

fig 31

Thread on 7A and pass up through the C and H bead again to make a second strap.

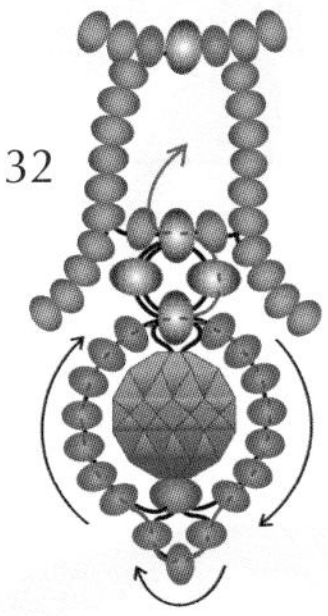

Referring to fig 32 pass the needle through the D on the ring, the 7A of the first strap, the 3A of the picot, the 7A of the second strap and the D bead once more to complete the frame. Pass through the D bead on the ring and the following 2D (fig 32).

fig 32

Pass the needle through the following 1E of the bridge, the beads of the swag and the foundation row to emerge from the D bead at the centre of the next 3-bead bridge and repeat Step 24.

Repeat Step 24 at the last 3-bead bridge to complete the beading over the bauble. Finish off this thread and all remaining thread ends neatly and securely.

25

The Hanging Loop - Prepare the needle as in Step 1 and thread on 2D and 1A.

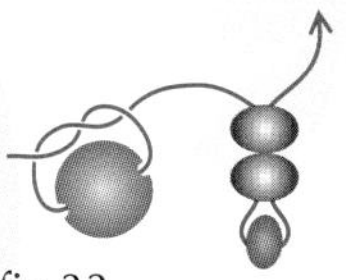

fig 33

Pass the needle back through the 2D beads to bring the A bead into an anchor at the end (fig 33).

Thread on 1K and 1J. Pass the needle back through the K bead to complete the body for a butterfly (fig 34).

The extra A bead at the bottom will provide a neat link for the sequence that connects to the bauble loop.

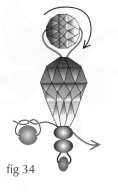

fig 34

26

Complete the butterfly wings as before but do not add any fringe strands. Finish with the needle emerging from the A bead at the bottom of the body.

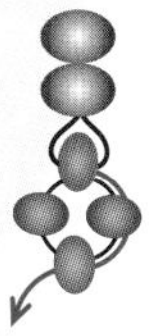

fig 35

Thread on 3E. Pass the needle through the A bead and the new 3E once more to make the link more firm. Pass through the 1A and first 2E beads (fig 35).

27

Thread on 1B, 1C and 1M. Pass the needle through the loop at the top of the bauble and back through the M, C and B beads.

Pass the needle through the E bead at the bottom of the link to centre the beadwork (fig 36).

Pass the needle through the beads just added twice more to strengthen the connection to the bauble.

fig 36

Pass the needle up through the beads of the link and the butterfly body to emerge from the J head bead.

Thread on 4E, 1B, 1L, 1C, 1B and 60E.

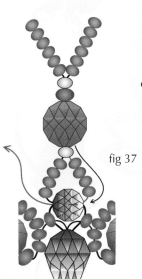

fig 37

Pass the needle down through the 1B, 1C, 1L and 1B beads to draw up the loop. Thread on 4E and pass through the J head bead (fig 37).

Pass the needle through the beads just added twice more to strengthen the loop and all of the connections.

Before finishing off this thread end pass the needle through the wing beads on this butterfly once more to stiffen the work. Finish off this thread end and all remaining ends neatly and securely.

Snow Queen Bauble

You Will Need

Materials

One 60mm frosted pale blue glass bauble
22g of size 10/0 silver lined crystal seed beads A
6g of size 8/0 silver lined crystal seed beads B
14g of pearl white Twin beads C
Twenty-five 6x4mm clear AB crystal rondelles D
Thirteen 8x6mm clear AB crystal rondelles E
White size D beading thread

Tools

A size 10 beading needle
A pair of scissors to trim the threads

see page 55 for the
Snowflake Strand decorations

Glittering crystal strands dangle from delicate snowflake motifs in a design fit for a palace of ice. Made with Twin beads these snowflake motifs come in two sizes, are quick to make and can be used in lots of different combinations.

The Decoration is Made in Five Stages

The six large snowflake motifs are made first.

A long fringe strand and a small snowflake is added to three of the large motifs.

The remaining three large snowflakes are decorated with three shorter fringe strands.

A fitted ring is added to the neck of the bauble which supports the prepared motif sets.

The hanging loop is added to the top of the bauble.

This design uses Twin beads - if you have not used them before see the technique notes on page 9.

1 The Large Snowflakes - Prepare the needle with 1.2m of single thread and tie a keeper bead 15cm from the end.

2 Thread on 6C. Pass the needle through the same hole on the first C bead again to make a ring of 6C (fig 1).

Pass the needle through the beads again to make the work firm - make sure you are passing through the same holes as before.

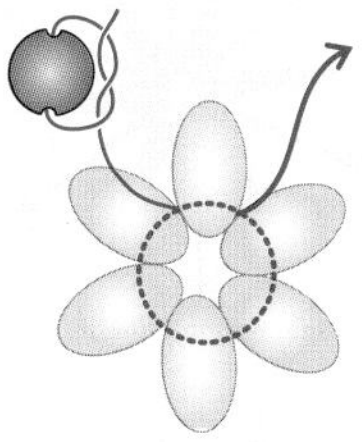

The needle is now transferred to the outer row of holes.

Following fig 2 pass the needle through the outer hole of the current C bead making a strap of thread on the side of the bead (fig 2).

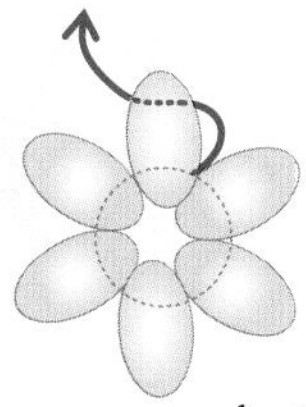

fig 1

fig 2

The next row is worked through the outer holes only.

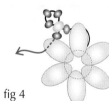

fig 3

fig 4

Repeat five times to add six picots in total (fig 5).

This completes a Small Snowflake motif - to make the Large Snowflake you need to add another two rows of beading.

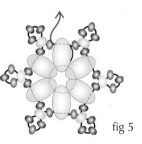

fig 5

3 Thread on 1A, 1B and 3A.

Pass the needle back through the B bead to bring the 3A into a picot (fig 3).

Thread on 1A and pass through the outer hole of the next C bead around (fig 4).

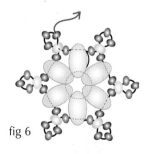

fig 6

4 The needle should be emerging from the outer hole on the first C bead (as fig 5) - it must be repositioned before you start the next row.

Referring to fig 6 pass the needle through the following 1A, 1B and 1A to point away from the centre of the motif.
The next row attaches to the A beads on either side of each picot.

Extra Info....
Making a spiky motif and working with Twin beads means the needle has to be repositioned for the next stitch with great care. If you skip across a gap or diagonally across the back of a Twin bead the work will twist and distort.
The extra thread passes build up the thread through the holes in the beads, which makes the work stronger and more sturdy. The motifs will hold their shape better which gives more design opportunities.

5 Thread on 1A, 1C, 1A, 1C and 1A.

Referring to fig 7 pass the needle down through the A bead on the side of the previous picot, the B bead below it and the following 1A, 1C, 1A and 1B.

Pass through the A bead on the opposite side of the first picot (fig 7).

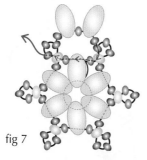

fig 7

6 Thread on 1A, 1C, 1A, 1C and 1A.

Following fig 8 pass the needle down the A bead on the side of the next picot around, through the B bead below it and the following 1A, 1C, 1A, 1B and the nearest A bead of the next picot around (fig 8).

fig 8

The needle is now positioned as in fig 6 (emerging from the A bead on the side of a picot ready to add the next stitch to the previous picot).

Repeat Steps 5 and 6 followed by another repeat of Step 5.

The last stitch, to complete the row, adds the same beads but the needle must emerge in a slightly different position.

7 Thread on 1A, 1C, 1A, 1C and 1A.

Following fig 9 pass the needle down the A bead on the side of the next picot around, through the B bead below it and the following 1A, 1C, 1A and 1B as before.

Now pass through the A bead on the far side of the next picot around and the following 1A, 1C, 1A and 1C (fig 9). Pass the needle through the outer hole of this C bead (as fig 2).

The next row attaches to the outer holes of the last row of C beads.

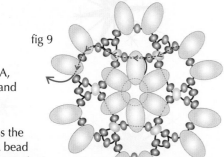

fig 9

8 Thread on 1A, 1B and 3A.

Pass the needle back down the B bead and thread on 1A.

Pass the needle through the outer hole of the adjacent C bead to make a picot as before (fig 10).

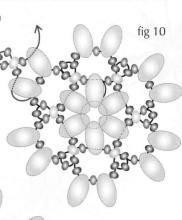

fig 10

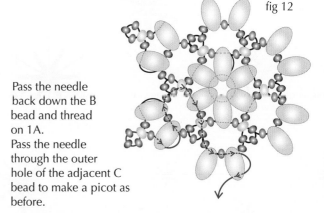

fig 11

9 Following fig 11, pass the needle through the inner hole of the current C bead and the following 1A, 1C, 2A, 1B, 1A, 1C of the first ring, 1A, 1B, 2A and the 1C, 1A, 1C of the next 2C around the motif.

Pass through the outer hole on this C bead to be ready to add the next picot (fig 11).

10 Referring to fig 12 throughout, thread on 1A, 1B and 3A.

fig 12

Pass the needle back down the B bead and thread on 1A.
Pass the needle through the outer hole of the adjacent C bead to make a picot as before.

Pass through the inner hole of this C bead and the following 1A, 1C, 2A, 1B, 1A, 1C of the first ring, 1A, 1B, 2A, 1C, 1A and 1C. Pass through the outer hole on this C bead ready to make the next picot (fig 12).

Repeat Steps 8, 9 and 10 twice to add the remaining picots to the last four pairs of C beads around the motif. Leaving the thread end loose, remove the needle.

Repeat Steps 1 to 10 five more times to complete a set of six Large Snowflake motifs.

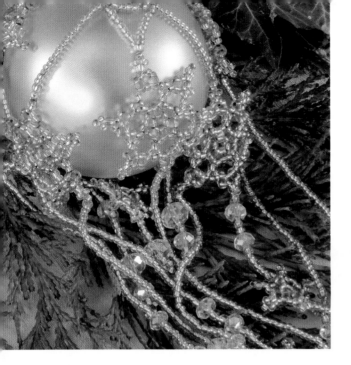

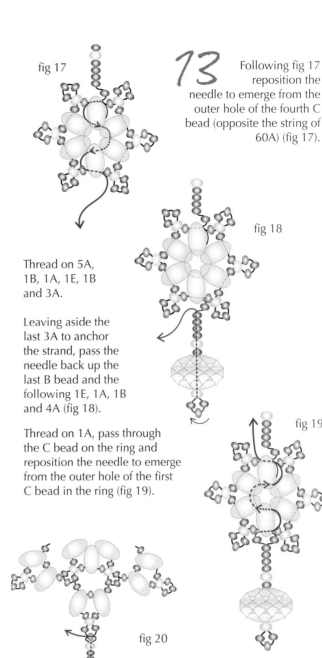

13 Following fig 17 reposition the needle to emerge from the outer hole of the fourth C bead (opposite the string of 60A) (fig 17).

fig 17

fig 18

Thread on 5A, 1B, 1A, 1E, 1B and 3A.

Leaving aside the last 3A to anchor the strand, pass the needle back up the last B bead and the following 1E, 1A, 1B and 4A (fig 18).

Thread on 1A, pass through the C bead on the ring and reposition the needle to emerge from the outer hole of the first C bead in the ring (fig 19).

fig 19

fig 20

60A total

14 Thread on 1A. Pass up through the second A above the C bead and the following beads to the edge of the large motif.

Pass through the A bead at the tip of the large motif in the same direction as before to centralise the strand below the picot (fig 20).*

Pass the needle through to the centre of the motif and finish off the thread end neatly and securely. Finish off any remaining thread ends on the motif similarly.

Repeat Steps 11 to 14 with two more of the Large Snowflake motifs and set aside for the moment.

11 The Long Fringe Strand Snowflakes - Select the motif with the longest thread end - is the thread at least 75cm long? If it is, attach the needle to this thread end. If not, attach a new 1m single thread to the motif.

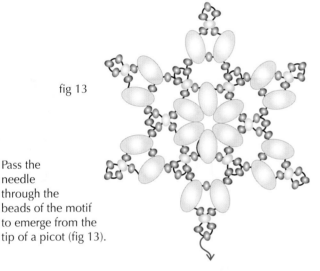

fig 13

Pass the needle through the beads of the motif to emerge from the tip of a picot (fig 13).

12 Thread on 1B, 60A, 1B, 1D, 1B, 1A, 1B, 1D, 1B, 1A, 1B, 5A, and 1C.

Pass the needle through the other hole in the C bead making a strap of thread on one side (fig 14).

fig 14

*Thread on 5C and pass through the same hole on the first C to make a ring as before (fig 15).

Pass the needle through the 6C once more to make the ring firm.

fig 15

fig 16

Pass the needle through the outer hole of this C bead (fig 16).

Repeat Step 3 to make this ring of 6C into a Small Snowflake motif.

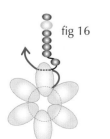

15

The Three Fringe Strand Snowflakes - Attach a new 1.2m thread to the fourth Large Snowflake motif to emerge as in fig 13 from the tip of a picot.

fig 21

Thread on 1B, 1D, 1B, 1A, 1B, 1D, 1B, 1A, 1B, 5A, and 1C.

Pass the needle through the other hole in the C bead making a strap of thread on one side (as fig 14).

Repeat from the * in Step 12 to the * in Step 14. Reposition the needle to emerge from the tip of the next picot point around the motif (fig 21).

16

Thread on 1B, 35A, 1B, 5A, 1B, 1D, 1B, 6A, 1B, 1A, 1E, 1B, 1A, 1D, 1B and 3A.

Leaving aside the last 3A to anchor the strand pass the needle back up through the last B bead and the following beads just added to emerge at the first B bead.

Pass the needle through the A bead at the tip of the snowflake picot in the same direction as before (fig 22).

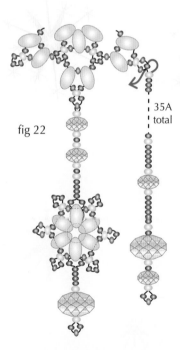

fig 22

35A total

Reposition the needle to emerge from the A bead at the tip of the picot on the other side of the small snowflake strand and repeat Step 16 (fig 23).

Finish off all thread ends neatly and securely.

Repeat Steps 15 and 16 twice to add three dangling strands to each of the last two Large Snowflakes.

fig 23

17

The Foundation Row - Thread on six repeats of 1B and 4A. Pass the needle through the first B bead again to bring the beads into a ring (fig 24).

Place the ring over the neck of the bauble - it needs to fit snugly so you may need to adjust the bead count.

fig 24

fig 25

If you need to make an adjustment, add or subtract A beads equally from all six sections to keep the B beads evenly spaced around the ring (fig 25).

Pass the needle through the beads again to make the ring firm. Remove the ring from the bauble.

18

The ring connects to the top picot on each of the prepared Large Snowflake motifs. The needle should pass through the A bead at the tip of the picot so the dangling strands are centralised below the motif.

You will start with a single strand motif followed by a three strand motif and repeat.

Thread on 9A and 1B.

Pass the needle through the top A bead at the tip of the first single strand Large Snowflake and back up through the B bead.

Thread on 9A and pass through the second B bead around the bauble neck (see fig 26).

fig 26

Thread on 20A and 1B.

Pass the needle through the top A bead at the tip of the first triple strand Large Snowflake.

Pass the needle back up through the B bead, the 20A above it and the B bead on the neck ring in the same direction (fig 26).

Repeat Step 18 twice more and finish off the thread ends neatly and securely.

19

The Hanging Loop - Repeat Steps 1, 2 and 3 to make a small snowflake motif. Finish with the needle emerging from a C bead as in fig 5.

Thread on 6A, 1B, 1E, 1B and 1A.

Pass the needle through the loop at the top of the bauble and back up through the 1A, 1B, 1E, 1B and the last 5A of the 6A just added (fig 27).

Thread on 1A and pass through the C bead on the snowflake as before.

Pass the needle through the beads of this connection to the bauble loop two or three more times to strengthen.

Reposition the needle to emerge from the outer hole on the opposite C bead.

fig 27

20

Thread on 6A, 1B, 1D, 1B and 50A.

Pass the needle back down the 1B, 1D, 1B and the first 5A of the 6A just added. Thread on 1A and pass through the hole in the C bead (fig 28).

Pass the needle through the beads of this connection and the loop two or three more times to strengthen.

Finish off all remaining thread ends neatly and securely.

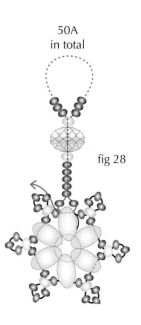

50A
in total

fig 28

Extra Info....

To properly exhibit the intricate outline of the large snowflakes the links to the foundation ring are kept very simple. This gives a very delicate and ethereal appearance when displayed on a frosted glass bauble.

If your bauble is handled or knocked whilst on display, the large snowflakes may slip out of place, skewing the weight distribution and making the decoration untidy. If you wish, you can add more stability by attaching six small straps to the support strands made in Step 18.

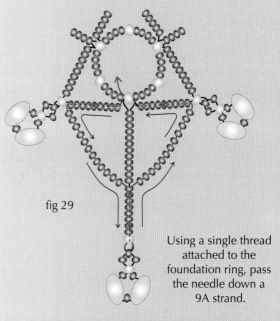

fig 29

Using a single thread attached to the foundation ring, pass the needle down a 9A strand.

Thread on 12A.

Pass the needle down the last 8A and 1B of the adjacent 20A strand, through the A bead at the tip of the picot and back up the 1B and 8A.

Thread on 12A and pass up through the next 9A strand around the neck (fig 29). Repeat twice more to add two small straps to each 20A strand.

Narcissa Bauble

You Will Need

Materials

One 60mm frosted lilac glass bauble
22g of size 10/0 silver lined crystal seed beads A
8g of size 8/0 silver lined lavender seed beads B
10g of size 3 silver lined crystal bugle beads C
Thirty-one 7mm crystal AB two-hole tile beads D
Twenty-four 6mm tanzanite fire polished faceted beads E
Thirty 4mm tanzanite fire polished faceted beads F
Eighteen 10x7mm crystal AB fire polished
faceted drops G
One 12mm clear AB fire polished faceted bead H
White size D beading thread

Tools

A size 10 beading needle
A pair of scissors to trim the threads

A cascade of narrow fringe strands weave, sparkle and fall all around this design. For its namesake, hang it in front of a mirror for double the design and twice the twinkle.

The Decoration is Made in Four Stages

A foundation row is fitted around the neck of the bauble.

Six loops are worked out from the foundation row - each loop supports a drop bead and two fringe strands.

Six further loops of seed beads are added in the gaps - each of these loops also supports two fringe strands. You will also add a second row of drop beads at this stage.

The hanging loop is added to the top of the bauble.

This design uses two-hole tile beads. If you have not used them before see the Extra Info boxes on pages 13 and 17.

1 The Foundation Row - **Prepare the needle with 1.5m of single thread and tie a keeper bead 15cm from the end.**

2 Thread on six repeats of 1B and 4A. Pass the needle through the first B bead again to bring the beads into a ring (fig 1).

fig 1

fig 2

Place the ring over the neck of the bauble - it needs to fit snugly so you may need to adjust the bead count.

If you need to make an adjustment, add or subtract A beads equally from all six sections to keep the B beads evenly spaced around the ring (fig 2). Remove the ring from the bauble.

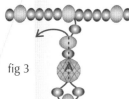

fig 3

3 The First Row of Loops - Thread on 1A, 1B, 1A, 1F, 1A, 1B and 1A.
Pass the needle back up the F bead and the following 1A and 1B (fig 3).

Thread on 1A, pass through the B bead on the ring and the first six beads just added to emerge from the B bead at the base of the strut (fig 4).

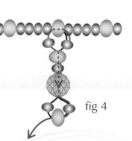

fig 4

4 Thread on 1B and pass through the B bead on the end of the strut to bring the holes in the two beads parallel. Pass the needle through the new B bead (fig 5).

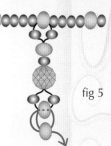

fig 5

Pass the needle through these two beads again to make a strong connection. Make sure you finish with the needle emerging from the new B bead as fig 5.

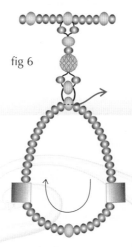

fig 6

5 Thread on 13A, 1D, 7A, 1B, 7A, 1D and 13A. Pass the needle through the previous B bead to make a loop (fig 6).

Pass the needle through the first 22 beads just added to emerge from the B bead at the bottom of the loop. This B bead supports the first two fringe strands.

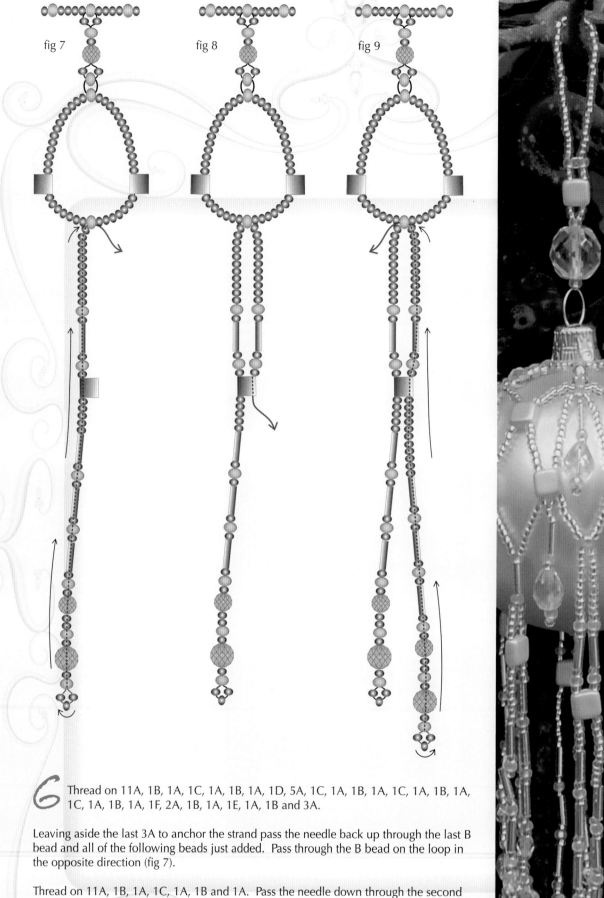

fig 7

fig 8

fig 9

6 Thread on 11A, 1B, 1A, 1C, 1A, 1B, 1A, 1D, 5A, 1C, 1A, 1B, 1A, 1C, 1A, 1B, 1A, 1C, 1A, 1B, 1A, 1F, 2A, 1B, 1A, 1E, 1A, 1B and 3A.

Leaving aside the last 3A to anchor the strand pass the needle back up through the last B bead and all of the following beads just added. Pass through the B bead on the loop in the opposite direction (fig 7).

Thread on 11A, 1B, 1A, 1C, 1A, 1B and 1A. Pass the needle down through the second hole in the D bead from the previous sequence (fig 8).

Thread on 11A, 1C, 1A, 1B, 1A, 1C, 1A, 1B, 1A, 1C, 1A, 1B, 1A, 1F, 2A, 1B, 1A, 1E, 1A, 1B and 3A. As before leave aside the last 3A to anchor the strand and pass back up through all of the beads just added. Pass through the B bead on the loop in the opposite direction (fig 9).

Pass through the following 22 beads of the loop to emerge from the B bead at the top of the loop.

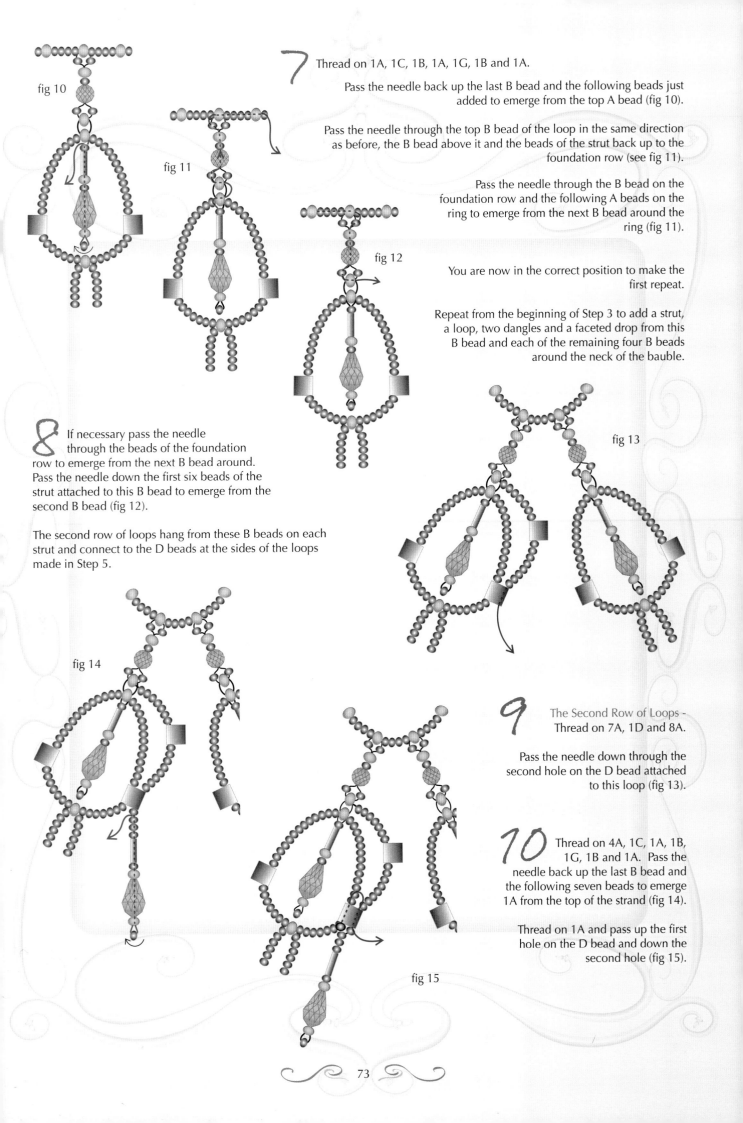

fig 10

fig 11

fig 12

7 Thread on 1A, 1C, 1B, 1A, 1G, 1B and 1A.

Pass the needle back up the last B bead and the following beads just added to emerge from the top A bead (fig 10).

Pass the needle through the top B bead of the loop in the same direction as before, the B bead above it and the beads of the strut back up to the foundation row (see fig 11).

Pass the needle through the B bead on the foundation row and the following A beads on the ring to emerge from the next B bead around the ring (fig 11).

You are now in the correct position to make the first repeat.

Repeat from the beginning of Step 3 to add a strut, a loop, two dangles and a faceted drop from this B bead and each of the remaining four B beads around the neck of the bauble.

fig 13

8 If necessary pass the needle through the beads of the foundation row to emerge from the next B bead around. Pass the needle down the first six beads of the strut attached to this B bead to emerge from the second B bead (fig 12).

The second row of loops hang from these B beads on each strut and connect to the D beads at the sides of the loops made in Step 5.

fig 14

9 The Second Row of Loops - Thread on 7A, 1D and 8A.

Pass the needle down through the second hole on the D bead attached to this loop (fig 13).

10 Thread on 4A, 1C, 1A, 1B, 1G, 1B and 1A. Pass the needle back up the last B bead and the following seven beads to emerge 1A from the top of the strand (fig 14).

Thread on 1A and pass up the first hole on the D bead and down the second hole (fig 15).

fig 15

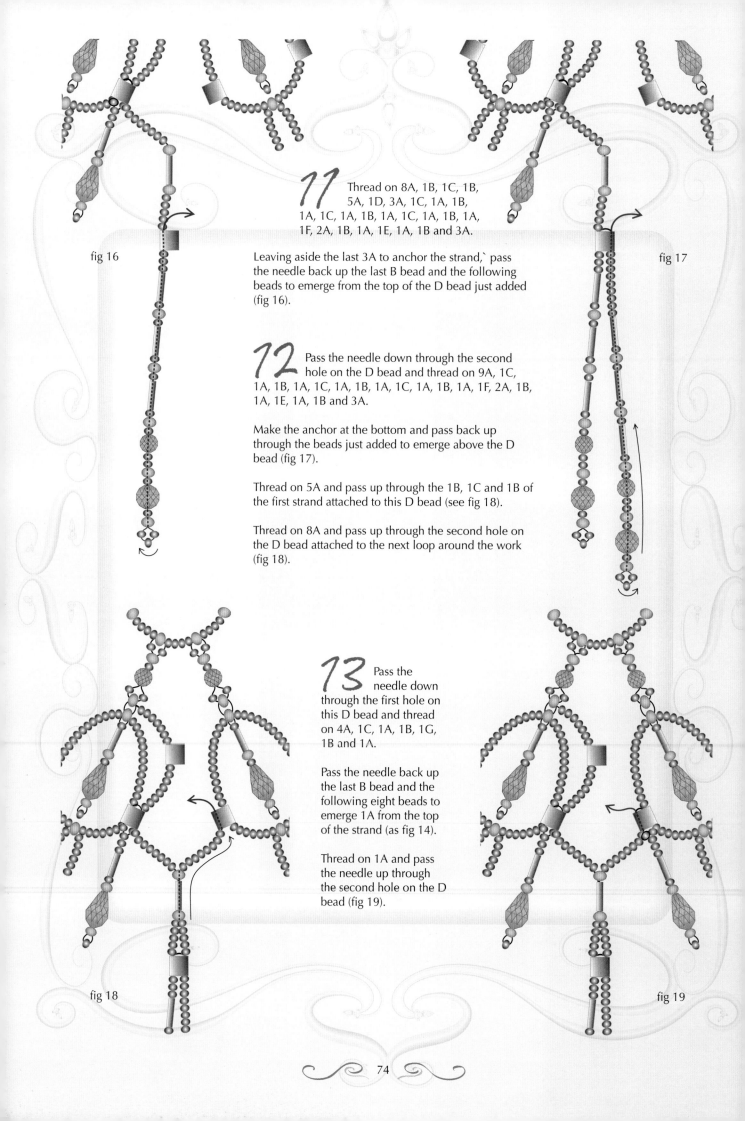

11 Thread on 8A, 1B, 1C, 1B, 5A, 1D, 3A, 1C, 1A, 1B, 1A, 1C, 1A, 1B, 1A, 1C, 1A, 1B, 1A, 1F, 2A, 1B, 1A, 1E, 1A, 1B and 3A.

Leaving aside the last 3A to anchor the strand,` pass the needle back up the last B bead and the following beads to emerge from the top of the D bead just added (fig 16).

fig 16

12 Pass the needle down through the second hole on the D bead and thread on 9A, 1C, 1A, 1B, 1A, 1C, 1A, 1B, 1A, 1C, 1A, 1B, 1A, 1F, 2A, 1B, 1A, 1E, 1A, 1B and 3A.

Make the anchor at the bottom and pass back up through the beads just added to emerge above the D bead (fig 17).

Thread on 5A and pass up through the 1B, 1C and 1B of the first strand attached to this D bead (see fig 18).

Thread on 8A and pass up through the second hole on the D bead attached to the next loop around the work (fig 18).

fig 17

13 Pass the needle down through the first hole on this D bead and thread on 4A, 1C, 1A, 1B, 1G, 1B and 1A.

Pass the needle back up the last B bead and the following eight beads to emerge 1A from the top of the strand (as fig 14).

Thread on 1A and pass the needle up through the second hole on the D bead (fig 19).

fig 18

fig 19

fig 20

14 Thread on 8A. Pass the needle up through the second hole on the D bead added in Step 9 and thread on 7A. Pass the needle through the B bead at the end of the next strut around the foundation row (fig 20).

You have completed the first loop of this pattern repeat and the needle is in the correct position to begin the second repeat.

Repeat from the beginning of Step 9 until you have completed all six loops. Finish off the thread ends neatly and securely.

15 The Hanging Loop - Prepare the needle with 1.2m of single thread and tie a keeper bead 15cm from the end.

Thread on 1H and pass the needle through the loop at the top of the bauble. Pass the needle back up the H bead (fig 21).

fig 21

Thread on 1B, 2A, 1D, 2A, 1B, 50A, 1B and 2A.

Pass the needle down the second hole in the D bead to pull the beads into a loop.

Thread on 2A and pass the needle down the first B bead to emerge alongside the keeper bead (fig 22).

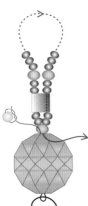

fig 22

Strengthen the connection to the bauble and the loop with at least two more passes of the needle before finishing off the thread ends neatly and securely.

Holly Wreath

★ ★ ★

This chapter makes a wreath ring 16cm in diameter resulting in a finished decoration approximately 25cm in diameter.
Each leaf measures 5-6cm long x 2.5cm wide and is supported on a 15mm stem.
The bow is 13cm tall and 11cm wide.

An adaptation of classic French techniques, these holly leaves are quick to master and very versatile. You can make garlands, napkin rings, candle sprays and perhaps a wintery tiara – espcially if you swap to a frosty white and silver palette.

You Will Need

Materials

35g of size 10/0 scarab green seed beads A
6g of size 10/0 silver lined dark gold seed beads B
35g of size 10/0 silver lined emerald seed beads C
6g of size 10/0 silver lined lime seed beads D
Eighteen 8mm red fire polished faceted beads E
Twenty one 6mm gold metallic sparkle beads F
25g of size 3 silver lined red bugle beads G
12g of size 10/0 silver lined red seed beads H
40m of 0.5mm leaf green soft tempered wire
18m of 0.315mm vivid red soft tempered wire
2m of 0.9mm leaf green soft tempered wire

Tools

A pair of wire cutters
A pair of flat nosed pliers
Masking tape or a similar non-marking tape

The Decoration is Made in Four Stages

The holly leaves are made first.
The berry clusters are made next.
The bow is made for the top of the wreath.
The wreath is assembled.

Extra Info....
Wire Twisting and Making Stamens

The wire is easy to control if you are precise when you make the twists.

Make a loop, of the specified size, crossing the wire over itself at the base (fig a).

Pinch the cross-over position firmly to stop the twist from travelling further along the wire.
Use your other hand to flip the loop over and over (fig b) to form the twist and produce a stamen with a small loop at the end (fig c).

The more firm you can make the pinch on the crossed wires: the easier it is to twist the wire.

Do not use pliers to grip or to twist the wire as the edge of the plier jaws can mark and scratch the coloured surface.

fig a

fig b

fig c

1 The Leaves - Cut 50cm of 0.5mm leaf green wire.

15cm from the end of the wire make a 6-7mm loop.

Referring to the Extra Info box (below left) pinch and twist to reduce the end loop to 2mm (fig 1). This twist will form the point and the tip of the leaf.

Separate the two ends of the wire.

fig 1

2 Thread 6A onto the shorter end of the wire and push up to the base of the twist.

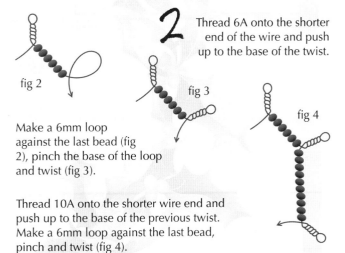
fig 2   fig 3   fig 4

Make a 6mm loop against the last bead (fig 2), pinch the base of the loop and twist (fig 3).

Thread 10A onto the shorter wire end and push up to the base of the previous twist. Make a 6mm loop against the last bead, pinch and twist (fig 4).

Repeat Step 2 on the longer end of the wire (fig 5).

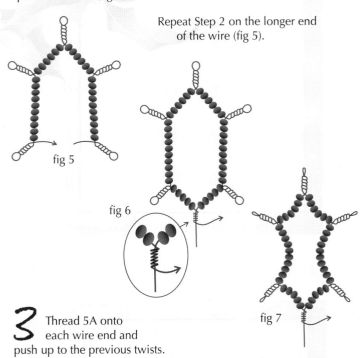
fig 5   fig 6   fig 7

3 Thread 5A onto each wire end and push up to the previous twists.

Wrap the longer wire end around the shorter wire five times to make neat parallel bindings immediately below the last beads (fig 6).

Manipulate the beaded sections between the twists to make a holly leaf outline with the twists pointing outwards. Align the loops to be in the opposite plane to the leaf outline (fig 7).

4 Working with the long wire end only thread on 8A. Push the beads down to the last binding. Pass the end of the wire through the first loop around the holly outline (fig 8).

Make a small bend in the wire against the loop to hold the beads up tight to the loop and to reduce any slippage (fig 9).

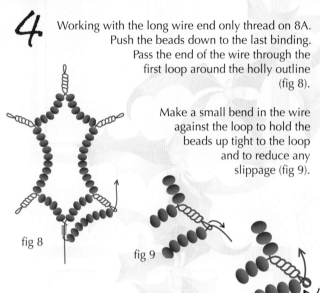

fig 8

fig 9

fig 10

Pass the end of the wire through the loop again. Pull the wire through slowly to tighten the new loop onto the old loop (fig 10).

Curve the 8A to replicate the outline of the 5A section.

5 Thread on 12A. Pass the end of the wire through the next loop around the holly outline and repeat figs 9 and 10 to tighten the new loop onto the old loop (fig 11).

Depending on the exact length of the twist supporting the next loop around, the bead count for the next section may need to be adjusted to make a good holly-like point. Thread on 8, 9 or 10A to form a curve to the loop at the leaf tip and attach as before.

fig 11

6 Continue the second row of the outline making the next section with the same bead count as the previous section and using 12A for the following section.

For the last section thread on 8A. Make one and a half parallel bindings around the short wire end immediately adjacent to the previous binding to complete the outline (fig 12).

fig 12

Make any necessary profile adjustment to the leaf outline to make the second row form a matching frame around the first.

7 Thread 20B onto the same long wire end. Lay this wire up the centre of the leaf to form the vein. There needs to be sufficient beads to reach the gap between the first leaf outline and the framing row (see fig 13) - you may need to add or subtract a few B beads to make it fit.

Bind the wire neatly into the gap with two parallel wraps and trim this wire end neatly. If necessary adjust the B bead line so it runs centrally from the stalk to the tip.

fig 13

8 Cut 20cm of 0.5mm leaf green wire. Bend this length in half and hook through the base of the leaf so the two ends lie parallel to the short wire stalk.

Referring to fig 14 pinch the three wires together 12-15mm from the base of the leaf and twist to the pinch point to form a more substantial 12-15mm stalk.

Leave the remainder of the wire ends untwisted as they will be easier to bind into the wreath in Steps 22 and 23.

Set the leaf aside for now.

Make a further seventeen leaves using the A and B beads.

Make nineteen leaves using C beads instead of A and D beads instead of B for the central veins.

fig 14

9 The Berries - Cut 30cm of 0.5mm leaf green wire.

Thread on 1E. Position this bead at the top of a 3cm loop in the centre of the wire. Pinch and twist to make a 2.5cm twisted stamen with the E bead at the top (fig 15).

fig 15

10 Thread 1E onto one side of the wire. Make a 3cm loop along-side the first stamen positioning the new E at the top of the loop as before.
Pinch the loop tightly closed against the base of the first stamen and twist to the pinch point (fig 16).
There should be no untwisted wire between the base of the two stamens.

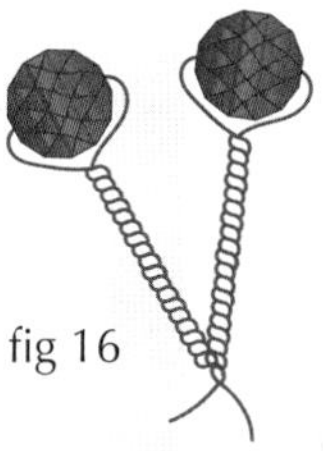

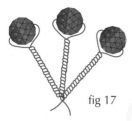

fig 16

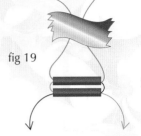

Thread 1E onto the other end of the wire and repeat to make a cluster of three E stamens (fig 17). Set the cluster aside for now.

Repeat to make five more stamen clusters of 3E and seven stamen clusters of 3F.

fig 17

11 The Bow - The bow is made with a simple cross-over weave technique. There are five sections to make - two separate Bow Loops, two Bow Tails and the Strap to wrap around the centre of the bow loops.

The Bow Loops - Read through the Extra Info box below and secure 1G, for the first row, to your work surface using 10cm of 0.5mm wire.

Cut 4m of 0.315mm red wire. Pass the end of the new wire through the G bead, bringing the two ends together, so the G bead is at the centre of the length - you have two 2m red wire ends to weave with.

Extra Info....
It is much easier to make a cross-over weave if the start of the work is anchored to your work surface.

Cut 10cm of 0.5mm wire and thread it through the first bead of the weave e.g. the first 1G of the bow loops.

fig d

Use a little masking tape to secure both ends of this short anchor wire to the work surface (fig d). Thread the weaving wire through this first row bead (fig e) and begin with row 2 of the sequence.

fig e

When the weave is complete remove the anchor wire.

Wire Breakage and Adding Wire to the Weave
If the wire breaks don't worry: you can add a new length. You need at least 5cm of loose end to finish off neatly so, if necessary, take out the last one or two rows. Both ends of the wire will need to be replaced to make a strong join, so trim the unbroken end to 5-8cm.

Cut a new length of wire and thread through the last row of the work so the row is central to the new wire and resume the weave. When you have worked a few rows return to the old wire ends. Pull the ends firmly and weave along the row edges as in fig 21 to secure.

12 Thread 1G onto one end of the wire and hold 10cm from the cut end.

Pass the other end of the wire in the opposite direction through this bead (fig 18 showing the two ends of the weaving wire in different colours).

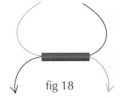

fig 18

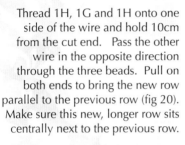

fig 19

Pull equally on both wire ends to bring the new bead up parallel to the first 1G (fig 19).

Smooth the last 15cm of each wire ready for the next row.

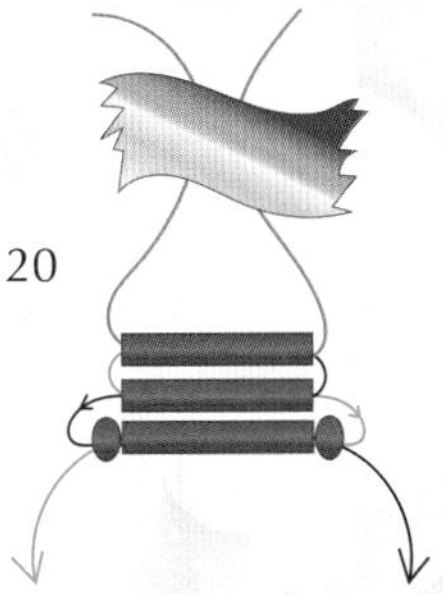

Thread 1H, 1G and 1H onto one side of the wire and hold 10cm from the cut end. Pass the other wire in the opposite direction through the three beads. Pull on both ends to bring the new row parallel to the previous row (fig 20). Make sure this new, longer row sits centrally next to the previous row.

Repeat to make another row of 1H, 1G and 1H.

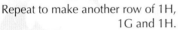

fig 20

This is the cross-over weave technique.

The wire will seem extremely long when you start but it reduces quickly as you work the rows. It's much better if you can work all the rows with one length but if you need to work with shorter lengths, or the wire breaks, see the Extra Info box (below left) for how to make a join.

13 Work the 25 rows shown in the two columns below making sure that each row is pulled up parallel and central to the previous row.

2H, 1G and 2H	2H, 3G and 2H
2H, 1G and 2H	2H, 3G and 2H
3H, 1G and 3H	3H, 3G and 3H
3H, 1G and 3H	3H, 3G and 3H
1H, 2G and 1H	1H, 4G and 1H
1H, 2G and 1H	1H, 4G and 1H
2H, 2G and 2H	2H, 4G and 2H
2H, 2G and 2H	2H, 4G and 2H
3H, 2G and 3H	3H, 4G and 3H
3H, 2G and 3H	3H, 4G and 3H
1H, 3G and 1H	1H, 5G and 1H. Repeat
1H, 3G and 1H	this row four more times.

The last five rows form the widest part of the bow loop. The shaping is now reversed.

Starting with two rows of 3H, 4G and 3H work the rows in the two columns above in reverse order.

Complete the shaping with two rows of 1H, 1G and 1H and two rows of 1G.

Remove the temporary anchor wire from row one.

14

The long edges of the weave need to be reinforced.

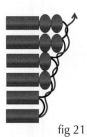

Along each long edge is a series of loops as the wire passes from one row to the next. Working along one edge at a time, with the attached wire end, whip stitch one loop to the next (fig 21).

When you reach the far end leave the ends *in situ* and set the bow loop aside for the moment.

fig 21

Repeat from Step 11 to make a second identical bow loop.

15

The Bow Tails - As before anchor 1G to your work surface with 10cm of 0.5mm wire.

Cut 3m of red wire and thread through the anchored 1G so it is in the middle of the new wire. Using the cross-over technique make the rows in the following two columns -

1G	
1H, 1G and 1H	1H, 3G and 1H
1H, 1G and 1H	2H, 3G and 2H
2H, 1G and 2H	2H, 3G and 2H
2H, 1G and 2H	3H, 3G and 3H
3H, 1G and 3H	3H, 3G and 3H
3H, 1G and 3H	1H, 4G and 1H
1H, 2G and 1H	1H, 4G and 1H
1H, 2G and 1H	1H, 2G, 1H, 2G and 1H
2H, 2G and 2H	1H, 2G, 1H, 2G and 1H
2H, 2G and 2H	1H, 2G, 2H, 2G and 1H
3H, 2G and 3H	1H, 2G, 2H, 2G and 1H
3H, 2G and 3H	The work now splits to
1H, 3G and 1H	make the points of the tail.

16

Thread 1H, 2G, 3H, 2G and 1H onto one side of the wire. Pass the other end through the last 1H, 2G and 1H only and pull the beads up to the previous row (fig 22).

You will work on this half of the tail point first.

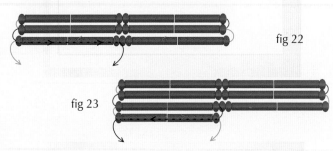

fig 22

fig 23

17

Thread 1H, 2G and 1H onto one wire end and cross the other end through as before (fig 23). Work the rows in the following two columns -

3H, 1G and 3H	5H
3H, 1G and 3H	4H
2H, 1G and 2H	3H
2H, 1G and 2H	2H
1H, 1G and 1H	Make the final row with 1H.
1H, 1G and 1H	Leave the wire ends attached.
6H	

18

Cut 1m of red wire. Thread it through the 1H, 2G and 1H on the other side of the last full width row so the beads are halfway along the new length (fig 24).

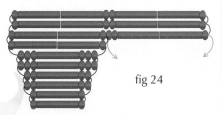

fig 24

Use these new wire ends to repeat Step 17 to complete the rows for the Bow Point.

Reinforce all the edges of the Bow Tail as in Step 14. Leaving the first row 1G bead unobstructed secure the ends of the wire with neat wraps and trim neatly.

Repeat from Step 15 to make a second Bow Tail.

The Bow Tails are now linked together and the Central Strap for the bow is created.

19

Cut 1.5m of red wire. Thread the first 1G row of each Bow Tail onto the new wire and position them at the centre of the length.

Thread 2H, 1G and 2H onto one wire end. Cross the other wire end through the new beads and pull up to the Bow Tails at the centre of the wire to make a triangle (fig 25).

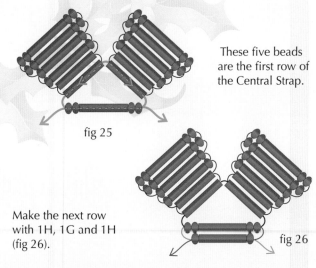

These five beads are the first row of the Central Strap.

fig 25

Make the next row with 1H, 1G and 1H (fig 26).

fig 26

Work the following sequence of rows -
1H, 1G and 1H - repeat this row eight times
2H, 1G and 2H - repeat this row seven times
1H, 1G and 1H - repeat this row four times.

20 Assembling the Bow - Gently fold each Bow Loop so row one (1G) sits parallel to the last row (1G).

Bring the two Bow Loops together overlapping the first and last 3-4 rows to make a four-layered stack at the centre of the arrangement (fig 27).

fig 27

Flatten this central section with your thumb so it is easier to hold. Use the wire ends still attached, or a new length of red wire if necessary, to secure the stack. A few stitches between the layers should suffice for the moment. Do not trim the wire ends yet.

You need to check the placement of the Bow Loops, the Bow Tails and the Central Strap before you secure them together.

Place the triangle at the top of the Bow Tails behind the stack so the points dangle down below the Bow Loops. The Central Strap will wrap over the front of the stack and the loose end will tuck in underneath the lower edge of the Bow Loops to make it neat. Adjust the arrangement until you are happy with the placement.

Return to the Bow Loops and re-secure the stack if necessary. Using the attached wire ends fix the triangle at the top of the Bow Tails to the reverse of the stack. Re-wrap the Centre Strap over the front to conceal all the previous connections and secure. Neaten and trim any wire ends less than 20cm long.

21 Assembling the Wreath - The 0.9mm wire is used to make the base for the wreath. Using the full 2m length make a continuous circle 16cm in diameter - 2m will make nearly four turns. Secure the circle with a tab of masking tape.

Using two or three 1.5m lengths of 0.5mm wire at once (for faster coverage) bind the circle all the way around to conceal the thicker wire and make a firmer base.

Place the circle on a piece of paper and draw around the outline. Allowing an 8cm gap for the bow, mark the remainder of the out-line into thirteen equidistant points. Each point is the approximate position for three leaves and a berry cluster - the first and last point will support just two leaves and a berry cluster, so as not to crowd the bow. As you work the next two steps refer back to this paper pattern to get your spacing nice and even.

22 The leaves and berries are attached first. The C bead leaves pair up with the F bead berry clusters and the A bead leaves with the E bead berries.

The first point - this marks the position for two C bead leaves and an F berry cluster. Each item needs to be attached separately. The wire tails all need to wind towards the second point around the circle and follow the same pitch (direction and angle) as the previous layer of binding around the ring.

Start with the F bead berry cluster. Offer it up so the bottom of the stamens touches the wreath base.

Make one wrap with the wire ends around the base (fig 28).

fig 28

23 Offer up the first C bead leaf so the bottom of the 12-15mm twisted stem comes up against the wreath base. Holding all the wire ends from the berries and the leaf together make one wrap around the wreath ring.
Offer up the second C bead leaf and repeat - this time you will be wrapping with the wire tails from all three items.

Continue winding, with all the wire ends, towards the second point following the same pitch as the previous binding. There is no need to trim any ends - just let them peter out and blend in as you go along.

When you reach the second point on your paper plan add in an A bead leaf, an E bead berry cluster and two A bead leaves using the same method.

Repeat around the base, according to your plan, to add the remaining leaves in alternating clusters of three leaves and a berry cluster.

Attach the bow to the wreath in the 8cm gap and arrange the leaves to suit, curving them this way and that, in a holly-like fashion.

Wise Owl Bauble

Twit-twoo ... an observant owl holding court between the branches of the Christmas tree. There's quite a bit of accurate counting and the needle has to be repositioned several times, so it's graded as a more difficult, but enjoyable project.

The Decoration is Made in Six Stages

The owl eyes and beak are made first using a combination of Brick stitch and Square stitch.

A foundation row is fitted around the neck of the bauble.

The first row of feather points are added to the foundation row.

The ears are added to the first feather row.

The remaining feather rows are made to connect the beak and eyes to the first feather row, cover the back of the bauble and make the wings which fold across the front of the design.

The hanging loop is added to the top of the bauble.

1 The Owl Eyes and Beak - Prepare the needle with 1m of single thread and tie a keeper bead 15cm from the end.

Thread on 1F. Pass the needle through the F bead again to make a strap on the side (fig 1).

Repeat to make a second strap on the other side of the F bead (fig 2).

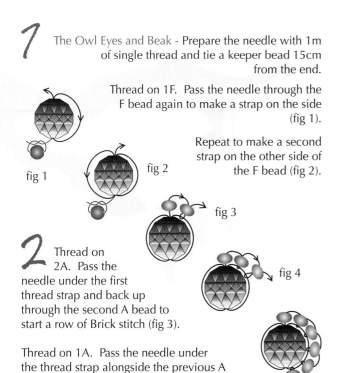

fig 1

fig 2

fig 3

fig 4

fig 5

2 Thread on 2A. Pass the needle under the first thread strap and back up through the second A bead to start a row of Brick stitch (fig 3).

Thread on 1A. Pass the needle under the thread strap alongside the previous A bead and back up the new A to make the first single Brick stitch (fig 4).

Make three more single A bead Brick stitches along this thread strap (fig 5).

3 Make five single A bead Brick stitches along the second thread strap. Pass the needle through the first A bead and the F bead to close up the row into a ring around the F bead (fig 6).

fig 6

Pass the needle through the closest A bead to emerge at the edge of the work. The next row of Brick stitch will attach to the thread loops between the A beads around the edge of the work.

4 Thread on 1E, 3D and 1E. Pass the needle under the first thread loop along and back up the second E bead to start the row (fig 7).

Thread on 3D and 1E. Pass the needle under the next thread loop along and back up the new E bead to make a single Brick stitch (fig 8).

Repeat this 3D and 1E stitch eight times.

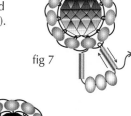

fig 7

Thread on 3D and pass the needle down the first E bead, under the thread loop and back up the same E bead to close up the circle (fig 9).

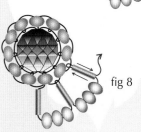

fig 8

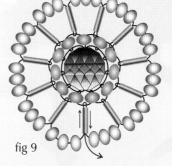

fig 9

Pass the needle through the D beads around the edge of the circle to bring them into line - do not pull the thread tight or the work will buckle.

Pass through the adjacent E bead to the inner A bead row and remove the needle.

Prepare the needle with 1.5m of single thread and repeat from Step 1 to make a second circle. Leave the needle attached.

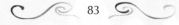

5 Before you move on you must line up the two circles, or eye discs, correctly. If the eye discs are out of alignment the face will appear crooked.

Examine the two eye discs - you can see where the first A bead on each disc lines up with the hole on the F bead. At the other end of the F bead there is 1A on either side of the hole - this end of the F bead should point towards the tip of the beak (fig 10 shows the alignment of the F bead holes in pink).

Arrange the eye discs as shown in fig 10 with the second eye disc (with the needle attached) to the left.

fig 10

Referring to fig 11 throughout, reposition the needle to emerge from the second E bead anti-clockwise from the lower F bead hole. Thread on 3D and pass through the corresponding E bead on the other eye disc.

fig 11

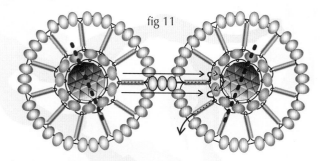

Reposition the needle to emerge from the end of the next anti-clockwise E bead around (fig 11).

6 Referring to fig 12 thread on 2D, 1H, 1G and 1C. Pass the needle back up the G and H beads to pull the C bead into an anchor.

Thread on 2D and pass the needle through the lower E bead on the first eye disc to make the arrangement symmetrical (fig 12).

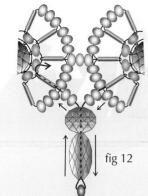

fig 12

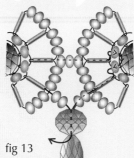

fig 13

Reposition the needle through the same A, E and D beads again to emerge between the H and G beads (fig 13).

7 The front of the H bead is covered with straps of A beads.

Thread on 5A and pass through the H bead to make a strap (fig 14). Repeat twice to make one strap on each side of the first strap.

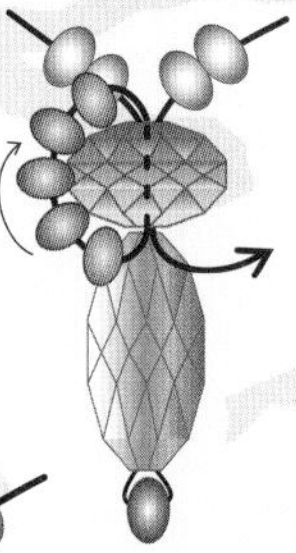

Thread on 4A and pass up through the last 1A of the previous strap. Pass down through the H bead (fig 15).

Thread on 4A and repeat passing up through the last 1A of the 5A strap on the other side of the central strap. Pass down through the H bead (as fig 15).

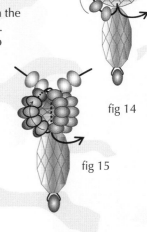

fig 14

fig 15

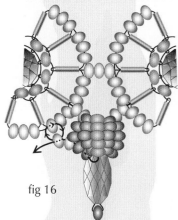

fig 16

8 Pass the needle up through the bottom 2A of the outermost strap on the left of the beak. Thread on 2D.

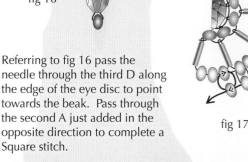

fig 17

Referring to fig 16 pass the needle through the third D along the edge of the eye disc to point towards the beak. Pass through the second A just added in the opposite direction to complete a Square stitch.

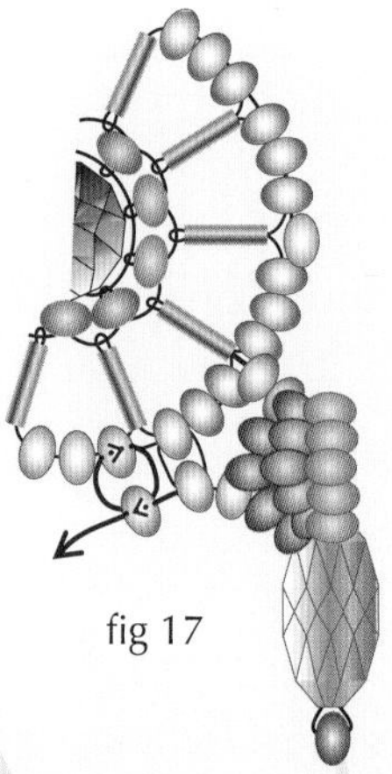

Thread on 1D. Square stitch this D to the next 1D along the edge of the eye disc (fig 17). Repeat to add two more single D bead Square stitches as fig 17.

9 Thread on 2D. Square stitch the second D just added to the next D bead along the edge of the eye disc to make an increase stitch (fig 18).

Work two single D bead Square stitches and one 2D increase stitch. Repeat this sequence of three stitches six times.

Make two single 1D stitches. The needle will be adjacent to the 3D added in fig 11.

fig 18

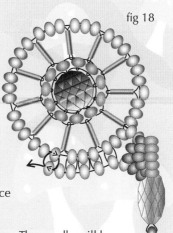

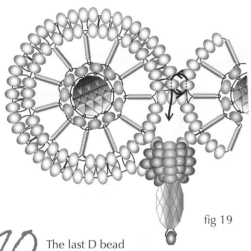

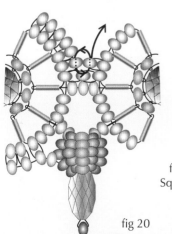

fig 19

10 The last D bead added has to be linked to the corresponding D bead on the other eye disc. Make a Square stitch to complete this link (fig 19).

Locate the central D bead of the 3D added in fig 11. Pass the needle through this D bead and back up through the last D bead added (to turn the needle to point upwards from the last D bead added).

Thread on 1D and Square stitch it to the next D bead around the second eye disc.

Link this new D bead to the adjacent D on the first eye disc with a Square stitch (fig 20).

fig 20

11 The second eye disc is now completed with a matching outer row of D beads. Make one single stitch followed by an increase stitch.

Make two single stitches followed by an increase stitch. Repeat this sequence six times.
Make three single stitches.

12 Thread on 1D and pass down through the bottom 2A of the adjacent beak row (fig 21).

Pass down through the G bead, the C bead at the bottom and up through the G bead.

Pass the needle through the bottom 2A of the beak row again to emerge at the start of the row just completed.

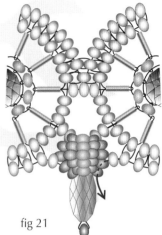

fig 21

Pass the needle through all the D beads of the second row to neaten - remember not to pull the thread too tight or the discs will buckle.

Finish off all the thread ends neatly and securely without blocking any holes in the D beads of the outer rows.

13 The Foundation Row - Prepare the needle with 1.5m of single thread and tie a keeper bead 15cm from the end.

Thread on nine repeats of 1B and 2A. Pass the needle through the first B bead to make a ring (fig 22).

Place the ring over the neck of the bauble - it needs to fit snugly so you may need to adjust the bead count.

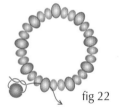

fig 22

If you need to make an adjustment, add or subtract A beads equally from all nine sections. If just a small adjustment is required add or subtract 1A from every third section - it is important to keep the 9B beads as evenly spaced as possible around the bauble neck.

Pass the needle through the beads of the ring again to make it firm - finish with the needle emerging from the first B bead as in fig 22. Remove the ring from the bauble.

14 The First Feather Points - Thread on 10A, 1B and 3A.

fig 23

Pass the needle back up the B bead to pull the last 3A into a picot (fig 23).

Thread on 10A and pass through the next B bead around the foundation ring. This is the centre front feather point which will sit above the owl face.

Thread on 1A and pass down through the ninth, eighth and seventh A beads of the 10A just added (fig 24).

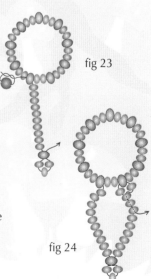

fig 24

15 Thread on 6A, 1B and 3C. Pass the needle back up the B bead to pull the last 3C into a picot (as fig 23). Thread on 10A and pass through the next B around the foundation row.

Thread on 1A and pass down through the ninth, eighth and seventh A of the 10A just added (as fig 24).

Repeat from the beginning of Step 15 six times to complete eight points.

The ninth point has to link to the centre front point made in Step 14.

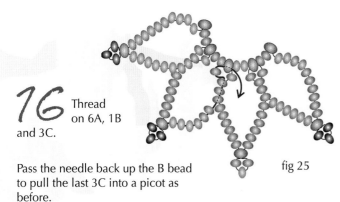

16 Thread on 6A, 1B and 3C.

Pass the needle back up the B bead to pull the last 3C into a picot as before.

Thread on 6A and pass up through the fourth, third and second A beads of the first 10A in Step 14. Thread on 1A and pass through the B bead of the ring (fig 25).

You have eight points with C bead picots and one point with an A bead picot.

fig 25

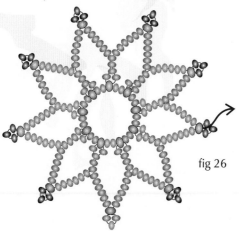

fig 26

Reposition the needle to emerge from the B bead pointing towards the picot on the third feather made (fig 26). This is the correct position to start the first ear.

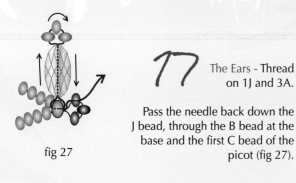

fig 27

17 The Ears - Thread on 1J and 3A.

Pass the needle back down the J bead, through the B bead at the base and the first C bead of the picot (fig 27).

18 Thread on 7A. Pass through the 3A beads at the top of the J bead and thread on 13A (see fig 28).

Locate the 2A beads between the B beads of the foundation row that support this feather point. If you made a bead count adjustment in Step 13 you may have a different A bead count here - treat your adjusted count as a block of 2A for the purposes of making The Ear.

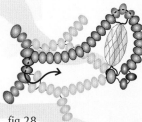

Pass the needle through the 2A on the foundation row (fig 28). Thread on 13A.

fig 28

Referring to fig 29, pass back through the closest 2A of the 3A at the top of the J bead to bring this strand parallel to the first 13A.

Thread on 3A. Pass through the last A of the previous 2A and the following 1A of the picot to emerge alongside the 7A (fig 29).

fig 29

Thread on 7A and pass through the third C bead of the feather point picot to bring this strand parallel to the first 7A (fig 30).

Pass the needle through the first C bead of the picot.

The paired strands are now Square stitched together.

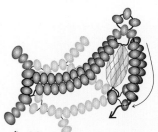

fig 30

side view

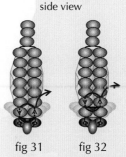

fig 31   fig 32

19 Pass the needle up the bottom 1A of the first 7A, down the adjacent A on the new 7A strand and back up the previous 1A (fig 31).

Repeat to link the next 1A on each strand together (fig 32).

Repeat five more times. Pass the needle through the 3A added in fig 29 and the following 1A of the first 3A stitch to emerge at the top of the 13A strands (fig 33).

Square stitch the first nine pairs of A beads together (as figs 31 and 32).

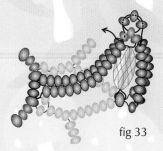

fig 33

Pass the needle down to the 2A beads of the foundation ring and through this 2A (or your adjusted bead count).

20 Reinforce the ear by passing the needle through the following 13A strand, the A beads of the ear tip and a 7A strand. Pass the needle back to the foundation ring through the other 7A and 13A strand.

Reposition the needle to emerge from the B bead on the eighth feather made (fig 34).

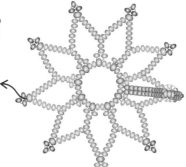

Making sure you are working on the top surface of the feather, complete a second ear to mirror the first.

Finish off the thread ends neatly and securely.

fig 34

21 Assembling the Remaining Feather Rows - The owl face sits beneath the 3A picot-tipped feather point from Step 14.

Attach a 1.5m single thread to the prepared face to emerge 10D from the top link between the eye discs (see fig 35).

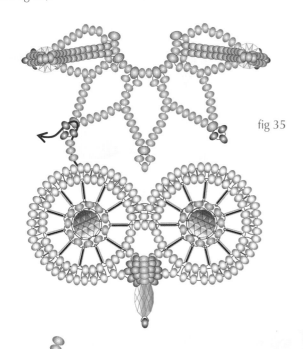

fig 35

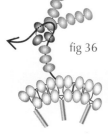

fig 36

Feather Row Two - Make sure the face is offered in the correct position with the 3A picot hanging between the eyes and the beaded surface of the beak facing outwards.

Referring to figs 35 and 36, thread on 3A and pass the needle up through the closest C bead of the adjacent 3C picot. Pass down the parallel C bead of the same picot (fig 36).

The first feather point of Row Two connects to the C beads supporting the ear.

22 Thread on 8A, 1B and 3C. Pass the needle back up the B bead to pull up a 3C picot and thread on 8A.

Pass the needle up the closest C of the adjacent 3C picot (supporting the ear) and down the parallel C bead (fig 37).

fig 37

Repeat Step 22 to attach the next feather point to the following 3C picot (fig 38).

Repeat to add five more feather points (including the fourth one along to the picot supporting the other ear).

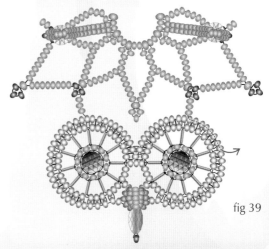

fig 38

23 Thread on 3A. Locate the eleventh D bead along the top edge of the other eye disc. Pass the needle through this D and the following 7D down the outer edge of the eye disc (fig 39).

fig 39

Extra Info....

Row Two has connected the eye discs to the first row of feather points. There are four more rows of feather points and the wings yet to be made.

These rows need to be connected to and work around the eye discs. The wings hang below the beak from the ends of the lower rows. You will find it useful to return the beading to the bauble at the end of each row – with the beading stretched out it will be easier to locate the correct connections.

Row Three is worked in the opposite direction around the bauble. It connects to the picots of Row Two and either side of the eye disc.

The first two swags (or strands) of the first wing are made next. These swags are long enough reach around to the centre front (just below the tip of the beak) and back to connect with last picot of Row Three.

Row Four is worked in the opposite direction around the bauble and connects to the picots of Row Three.

The first two swags of the second wing are made next – the tip of this wing connects to the first wing at the centre front just below the beak tip.
The second two swags of this wing are added, allowing the needle to be repositioned for Row Five.

Row Five is worked in the opposite direction around the bauble and connects to the picots of Row Four.

The second two swags of the first wing are added to make the wings symmetrical.

Row Six is worked in the opposite direction around the bauble and connects to the picots of Row Five.

fig 40

24 Row Three - Thread on 3A, 1B and 3C. Pass the needle back up the B bead to make the picot and thread on 8A.

Locate the last picot made on Row Two.

Pass up through the closest C and down through the parallel C of this picot (fig 40).

Note you are working in the opposite direction around the bauble.

25 Thread on 8A, 1B and 3C. Make the picot and thread on 8A. Pass the needle up the closest C and down the parallel C of the next 3C picot along the previous row (as before). Repeat five more times.

The last feather point of the row attaches to the adjacent edge of the eye disc (to mirror the start of the row).

Thread on 8A, 1B and 3C. Make the picot and thread on 3A. Locate the ninth D bead down the edge from the last strand attachment on the eye disc and pass the needle down through this bead (towards the beak).

26 The First Wing - The top two rows of the wing on this side of the centre front are made next - this enables you to turn the needle for the fourth row of feather points.

Thread on 1A and Square stitch to the next D bead along the edge of the eye disc (fig 41).

Repeat to add six more 1A Square stitches to the next 6D along.

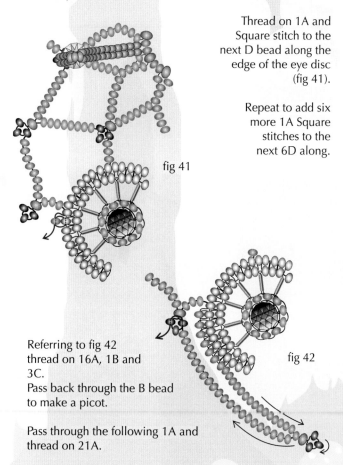

fig 41

fig 42

Referring to fig 42 thread on 16A, 1B and 3C.
Pass back through the B bead to make a picot.

Pass through the following 1A and thread on 21A.

Locate the last picot of Row Three.
Pass up through the closest C bead of this picot and down through the parallel C bead ready to begin the fourth row (fig 42).

27 Row Four - Thread on 10A, 1B and 3C. Make a picot and thread on 10A. Connect to the previous picot of Row Three as before.

Repeat to complete Row Four with six more feather points.

Finish with the needle pointing upwards from the first C of the last picot connection. The needle now has to be repositioned to start the second wing.

28 Referring to fig 43 pass up through the following 1B and the 3A link to the side of the eye disc.

Pass down through the following 1D along the edge of the eye disc (towards the beak as before) (fig 43).

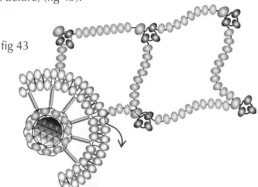

fig 43

29 The Second Wing - Thread on 1A and square stitch to the next D bead along the edge of the eye disc (as fig 41). Repeat to add six more 1A Square stitches to the next 6D along.

Thread on 16A to start the first wing swag on this side of centre front. Referring to fig 44 thread on 1B, 2C and 1A.

fig 44

Pass the needle through the middle C bead of the picot at the tip of the first wing (fig 44).

Referring to fig 45 thread on 1A and pass through the last C bead added in the opposite direction.

fig 45

Thread on 1C, pass back through the new B bead and the following 1A to complete the picot (fig 45).

30 Thread on 22A. Pass the needle through the B bead of the wing picot just made in fig 45, the 3C of the picot and back through the B bead. Pass back through the last 6A added (fig 47).

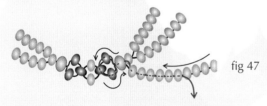

fig 47

Thread on 16A for the fourth wing swag. Locate the last picot made on Row Four. Pass the needle up through the closest C bead of this picot and the following 1B and 5A towards the eye disc. The needle will emerge at the top of the previous wing swag (fig 48).

Thread on 21A.

To match the other side of the design this swag has to connect back to Row Three.

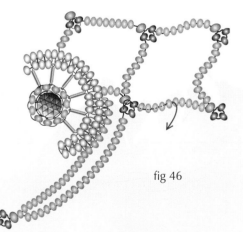

fig 46

fig 48

Referring to fig 46, pass the needle up through the closest C on the last picot of Row Three. Pass down the parallel C and the first 5A of the following feather point (fig 46).

The third wing swag starts from this position.

33

Referring to fig 52 pass the needle through the first 3A of the previous feather and the following 8A of the lower wing edge (fig 52).

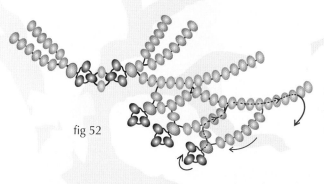

fig 52

Thread on 7A, 1B and 3C. Make the picot and thread on 1A.

As before complete the point by passing through the first 3A of the previous feather and the following 8A of the fourth swag to emerge adjacent to the last picot point of Row Four (fig 53).

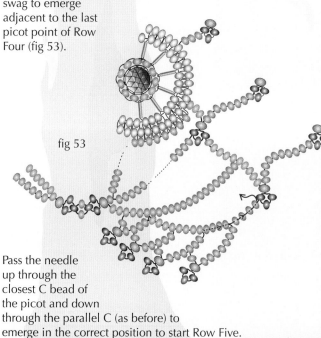

fig 53

Pass the needle up through the closest C bead of the picot and down through the parallel C (as before) to emerge in the correct position to start Row Five.

31

Completing the Wing - The lower edge of the wing (the fourth swag) is decorated with four small feather points. The needle has to be repositioned before these feather points can be added.

Pass the needle down through the 22A of the third swag of the wing. Referring to fig 49 pass the needle through the following 1B, the 3C of the picot and back through the B bead. Pass through the first 6A back along the third swag to emerge at the start of the fourth swag (fig 49).

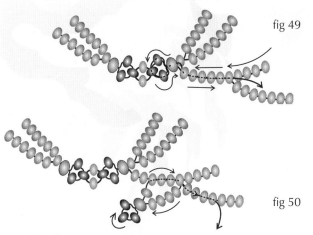

fig 49

fig 50

32

The Small Feather Points - Thread on 4A, 1B and 3C. Make the picot as before and thread on 1A. Referring to fig 50 pass the needle through the preceding 4A of the third swag and the following 4A of the fourth swag (fig 50).

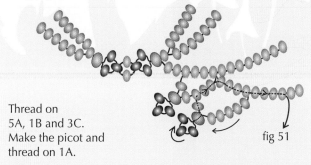

Thread on 5A, 1B and 3C. Make the picot and thread on 1A.

fig 51

Referring to fig 51 pass the needle through the first 3A of the previous feather and the following 8A of the fourth swag (fig 51).

Thread on 6A, 1B and 3C. Make the picot and thread on 1A.

34 Row Five - Using a bead count of 10A above the picot (as in Row Four) make six feather points to connect to the seven picot points of Row Four. Finish with the needle pointing upwards from the first C of the last picot connection.

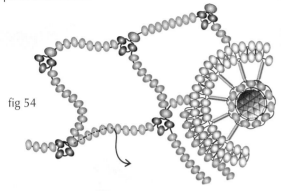

fig 54

Referring to fig 54 pass up through the following 1B and 5A towards the eye disc. The third swag of the wing on this side of the centre front starts from this position.

(See also fig 46 which shows the needle emerging from the same gap between the A beads but on the opposite side of the design.)

Repeat Steps 30 to 33 to complete a matching wing on this side of the owl.

35 Row Six connects to the picots of Row Five. At present the needle is emerging alongside the last picot of Row Four.

Referring to fig 55 reposition the needle to emerge from the last picot of Row Five (fig 55).

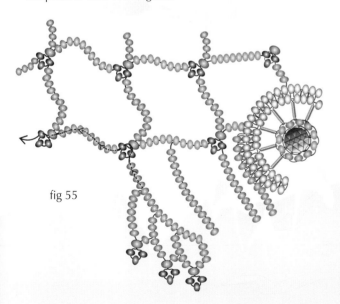

fig 55

Row Six - Thread on 10A, 1K, 1B and 3C.
Pass back up through the B and K beads to make the picot.
Thread on 10A and link to the next picot along Row Five as before.

Repeat to the end of the row (five feather points in total).

Finish off all the thread ends neatly and securely.
Place the beading over the bauble.

Elton the Owl

A very cute simplification of the Wise Owl design made on a 30mm bauble.

The eye discs are made from three rows of Brick stitched seed beads around two 4mm faceted beads. The beak is an 11x3mm dagger bead.

The main netted cover is made separately with two simple swags inserted at the centre front.

The ears are created using two more 4mm facets.

The eye discs are stitched to the front of the completed net and a hanging loop is added to the top.

36 The Hanging Loop - Prepare the needle with 1m of single thread and tie a keeper bead 15cm from the end.

Thread on 1L, 1C, 1B and 1C. Pass the needle through the loop at the top of the bauble and pass back up through the beads just added.

Thread on 1C, 1B, 1C and 50D. Pass the needle back down the last 1C, 1B and 1C threaded to pull up the loop (fig 56).

Pass the needle through the beads of the connection to the bauble and the loop at least three more times to strengthen the work.

Finish off both thread ends neatly and securely.

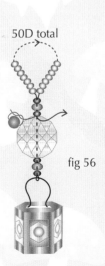

50D total

fig 56

Wenceslas Bauble

You Will Need

Materials

One 60mm frosted purple glass bauble
10g of size 10/0 silver lined purple seed beads A
15g of frost metallic gold Twin beads B
3g of size 10/0 frost metallic gold seed beads C
15g of size 8/0 frost metallic gold seed beads D
Twenty-one 6mm teal AB fire polished faceted beads E
Seven 6mm purple fire polished faceted beads F
Seven 8mm red fire polished faceted beads G
Fourteen 4mm red fire polished faceted beads H
Seven 4mm teal AB fire polished faceted beads J
One 12mm red fire polished faceted bead K
Purple size D beading thread

Tools

A size 10 beading needle
A pair of scissors to trim the threads

Building on the opulence of the Prague Bauble, the Wenceslas design adds more grandeur with jewelled cartouches and a regal crown. The Bohemian King would surely approve of this spectacular use of beads made in his ancestral homeland.

The Decoration is Made in Seven Stages

The fringe strands are made as separate units before being brought together with a series of loops from the neck of the bauble.

The seven long fringe strands attached to the G bead cartouches are made first.

The seven shorter fringe strands are made second.

A foundation row to fit around the neck of the bauble is made next.

The G bead cartouche strands are linked to the foundation row.

The G bead cartouches are linked together with swags that support the shorter fringe strands.

The crown is made for the top of the bauble and attached to the foundation row.

The hanging loop is attached to the top of the bauble to complete the design.

1
The Long Strands - The G bead cartouche (ornate frame) is made first.

Prepare the needle with 1.2m of single thread and tie a keeper bead 15cm from the end.

Thread on 1G, 3D, 1B, 1D and 1B. Pass the needle through the G bead to bring the smaller beads into a strap at the side (fig 1).

Thread on 3D, 1B, 1D and 1B. Pass the needle through the G bead again to make a second strap.

fig 1

2
Pass the needle through the six beads of the first strap and thread on 2B. Pass through the following six beads of the second strap (fig 2).

Thread on 2D and pass through the beads of the first strap again (fig 3).

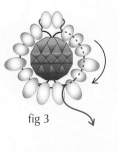

fig 3

fig 2

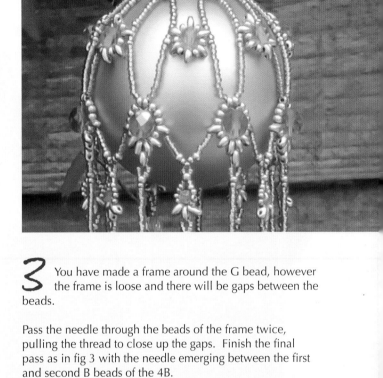

3
You have made a frame around the G bead, however the frame is loose and there will be gaps between the beads.

Pass the needle through the beads of the frame twice, pulling the thread to close up the gaps. Finish the final pass as in fig 3 with the needle emerging between the first and second B beads of the 4B.

The G bead will 'pop' to one side of the frame making a prominent dome on the front of the motif: the back of the motif will be relatively flat. When you assemble the design in Step 19 you will need to make sure that the domed fronts of the motifs all show on the outside of the design.

4
Reposition the needle by passing through the following 2B beads of the frame and the outer hole of the current B bead to emerge between the middle 2B.

Thread on 1B and pass through the outer hole of the following 1B (fig 4).

fig 4

Referring to fig 5 pass back through the inner holes of the two middle B, the outer hole of the current B and the hole in the new B bead.

Pass through the outer hole in this new B bead.

fig 5

Extra Info....

The first cartouche (ornate frame) is now complete - the long strand will hang from the current B bead.

It is important that you DO NOT use an overly firm tension during the next few steps. The long strand must remain flexible and the lower motif needs to hang centrally from the bottom of the strand (not pull to one side or the other).

5

Thread on 2A, 1D, 1C, 18A, 1D, 1J, 1D, 3A, 2D, 1H and 2D.

Pass the needle through the 2D before the H bead and the H bead. This brings the 2D threaded on either side of the H bead together to form a strap around the top of the H bead (fig 6).

fig 6

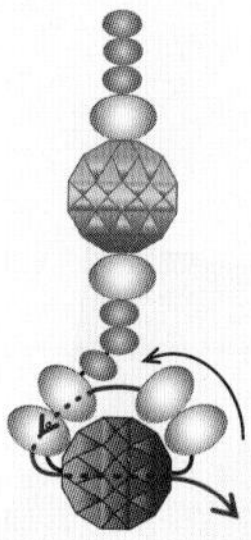

Thread on 1D, 2B and 1D. Pass the needle through the H bead again (fig 7).

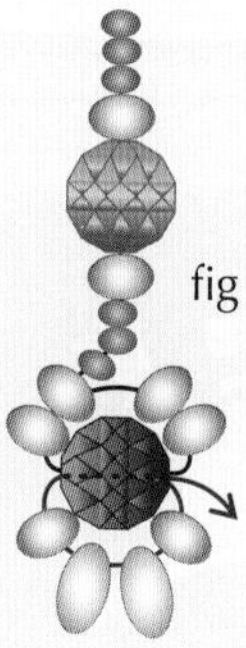

fig 7

6

Pass the needle through the first 4D strap and thread on 1D.

Pass the needle through the 1D, 2B and 1D just added to pull the new D bead into the gap (fig 8).

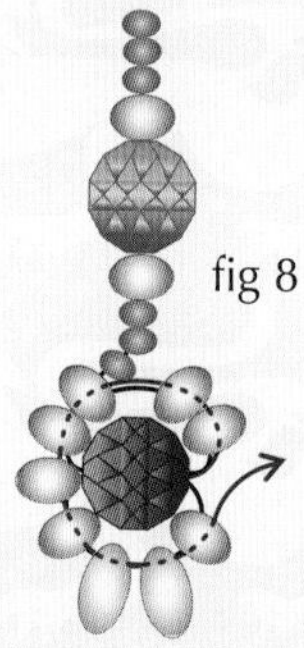

fig 8

Thread on 1D and pass the needle through the first 4D strap again (fig 9). Pass through the following 2D and 2B.

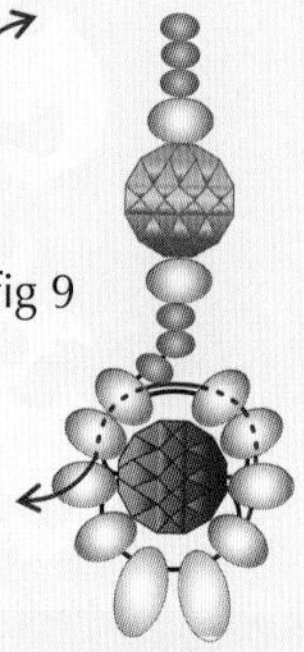

fig 9

Pass the needle through the outer hole of the current B bead to emerge between the 2B beads (fig 10).

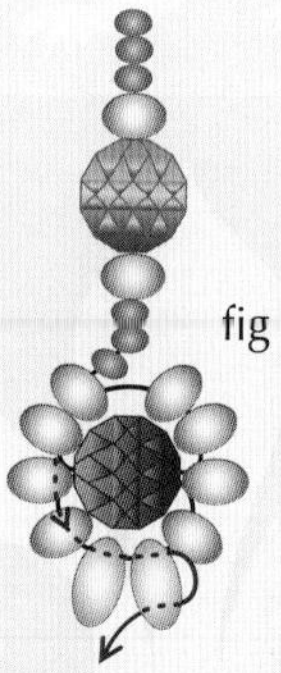

fig 10

7

Thread on 1B.

Pass through the outer hole of the following B bead (fig 11).

fig 11

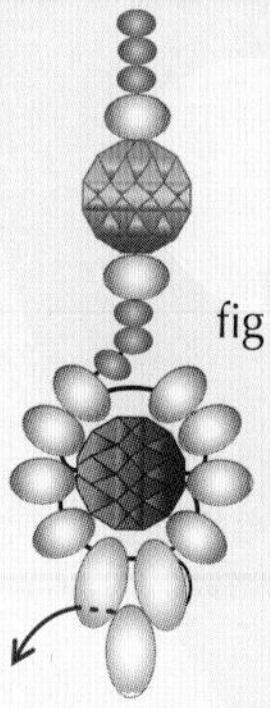

Referring to fig 12 pass the needle through the inner holes of the original 2B, the outer hole of the first B, the following hole of the new B and the outer hole of the new B to reposition the needle for the last section of the strand.

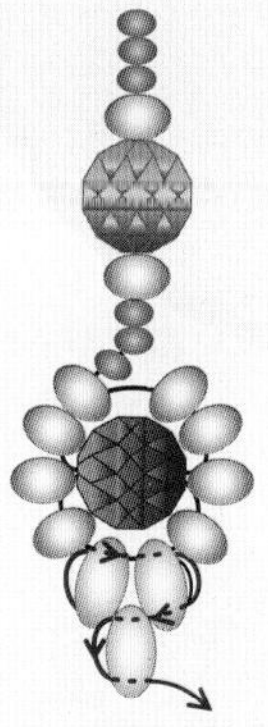

fig 12

8

Thread on 3A, 1C, 1A, 1E, 1A, 1D and 3A.

Leaving aside the last 3A to anchor the strand, pass the needle back up the D bead and the following 1A, 1E, 1A and 1C (fig 13).

fig 13

Thread on 3A and pass through the outer hole of the B bead to centralise the strand end (fig 14).

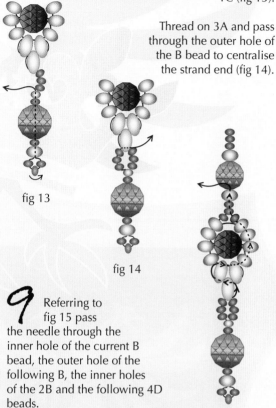

fig 14

9

Referring to fig 15 pass the needle through the inner hole of the current B bead, the outer hole of the following B, the inner holes of the 2B and the following 4D beads.

Thread on 1A and pass up the 2A and 1D below the J bead on the main strand (fig 15).

fig 15

Make sure that the H bead motif is hanging straight below the main strand.

Pass the needle up through the following 1E, 1D, 18A, 1C and 1D.

Thread on 2A and pass through the outer hole of the middle B bead of the G bead cartouche (fig 16).

fig 16

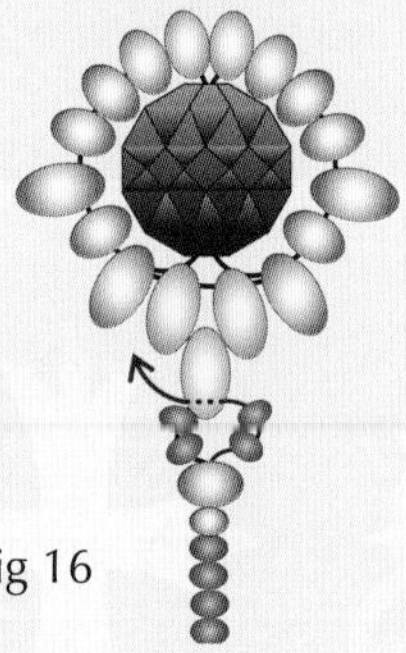

Pass through the inner hole of the same B bead.

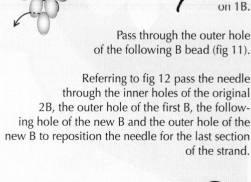

This completes the beading for the long strand.

Remove the keeper bead and finish off this short thread end neatly and securely without blocking the holes in the G bead cartouche.

Leave the long thread end attached. Set the strand aside.

Repeat from Step 1 to Step 9 six times to make seven long strands in total.

10 The Short Strands - A cartouche frame around an F bead is made first. Prepare the needle with 1m of single thread and tie a keeper bead 15cm from the end.

Thread on 1F and 4D. Pass the needle through the F bead to bring the 4D into a strap at the side (fig 17).

Thread on 4D and repeat to make a second strap.

fig 17

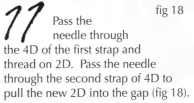

fig 18

11 Pass the needle through the 4D of the first strap and thread on 2D. Pass the needle through the second strap of 4D to pull the new 2D into the gap (fig 18).

fig 19

Thread on 2B and pass the needle through the 4D of the first strap and the first 1D of the 2D just added (fig 19).

fig 20

12 Thread on 4C. Leaving aside the last 3C beads, pass the needle back through the first C bead and through the following 1D to make a picot (fig 20).

Pass the needle through the following 4D and 2B around the F bead.

Pass the needle through the outer hole of this B bead to emerge between the B beads (fig 21).

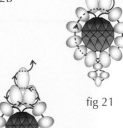

fig 21

Thread on 1B and pass the needle through the outer hole of the following B bead.

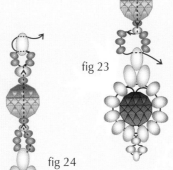

fig 22

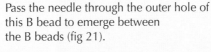

fig 23

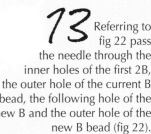

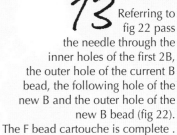

13 Referring to fig 22 pass the needle through the inner holes of the first 2B, the outer hole of the current B bead, the following hole of the new B and the outer hole of the new B bead (fig 22). The F bead cartouche is complete.

fig 24

Thread on 3A, 1C, 1A, 1E, 1A, 1D, 2A, 1B and 2A. Pass the needle back through the previous D bead and the following 1A, 1E, 1A and 1C (see fig 23).

Thread on 3A and pass through the outer hole of the B bead to centre the beads just added above the F bead cartouche (fig 23).

Pass the needle back up through the beads above the cartouche to emerge from the outer hole of the B bead at the top (fig 24).

14 Thread on 1B, 1C, 1H, 1C and 1B. Pass the needle through the outer hole of the B bead at the top of the link (fig 25).

Pass through the following 1B, 1C and the H bead.

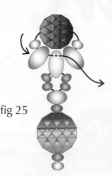

fig 25

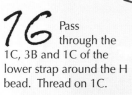

fig 26

15 Thread on 2C, 1A, 1D and 3A.

Leaving aside the last 3A beads, pass back through the D bead to make a picot.

Thread on 1A and 2C and pass through the H bead (fig 26).

fig 27

16 Pass through the 1C, 3B and 1C of the lower strap around the H bead. Thread on 1C.

Pass through the following 2C, 1A, 1D and the 3A of the picot.
Pass back down the D bead and the following 1A and 2C (fig 27).

Thread on 1C and pass through the following 1C and 2B to complete the frame around the H bead.

fig 28

Pass through the other hole of the current B bead, through the beads of the link and the F bead frame to emerge alongside the keeper bead (fig 28).

Make sure the motifs at either end of the link are in line and finish off both thread ends neatly and securely.

Repeat Steps 10 to 16 six more times to make seven short links in total.

17 The Foundation Row - Prepare the needle with 1.5m of single thread and tie a keeper bead 15cm from the end.

Thread on seven repeats of 1B and 3A. Pass the needle through the same hole on the first B bead again to make a ring (fig 29).

Place the ring over the neck of the bauble - it needs to fit snugly without the thread showing between the beads.

fig 29

fig 30

If the fit is not good, remove the ring and rethread with seven repeats of 1B and 4A (or to make it smaller use 1B and 2A). The seven B beads must be equally spaced around the bauble neck (fig 30).

Remove the ring from the bauble and pass the needle through all the beads again to make the ring firm. Make sure the needle is emerging from the first B bead as shown in fig 29.

Pass the needle through the outer hole of the first B bead to move to the outer edge of the ring.

18 Linking the Large Cartouches - Thread on 1A, 1C, 1A, 1B, 1A, 1C and 1A.

Pass the needle through the outer hole of the next B bead around the ring (fig 31).

Repeat six more times to complete seven small loops.

fig 31

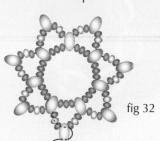

fig 32

Pass the needle through the following 1A, 1C, 1A and 1B of the first loop just made.

Pass through the outer hole of this B bead to be in the correct position for the next step (fig 32).

19

Thread on 9A, 1C, 1A, 1B, 1A, 1C and 12A.

Pick up the first long strand made in Steps 1-9 and locate the 2D beads added in fig 3.

Pass the needle through these 2D and thread on 12A, 1C, 1A, 1B, 1A, 1C and 9A. Pass the needle through the B bead on the small loop from Step 18 (fig 33).

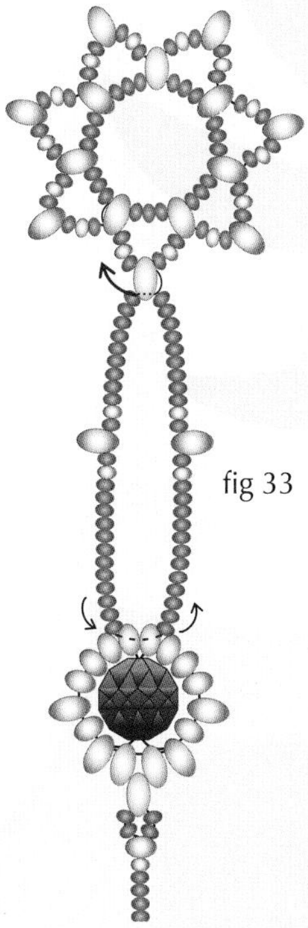

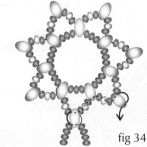

fig 33

fig 34

Pass the needle through the other hole in this B bead and the following 1A, 1C, 1A, 1B, 1A, 1C, 1A and 1B. Pass the needle through the outer hole of this B bead to be in the correct position to start the next connecting loop (fig 34).

Remembering to check that the domed centre of each G bead cartouche is facing outwards, repeat Step 19 six more times to add the remaining six large cartouche strands to the work.

Finish with the needle emerging from the outer hole of the B bead at the top of the first long loop (as fig 33).

20

Pass down through the first 9A, 1C, 1A and 1B of the attached long strand.

Pass up through the other hole of this B bead (fig 35).

This B bead and the adjacent B bead from the previous strand are now linked together to make a new cartouche.

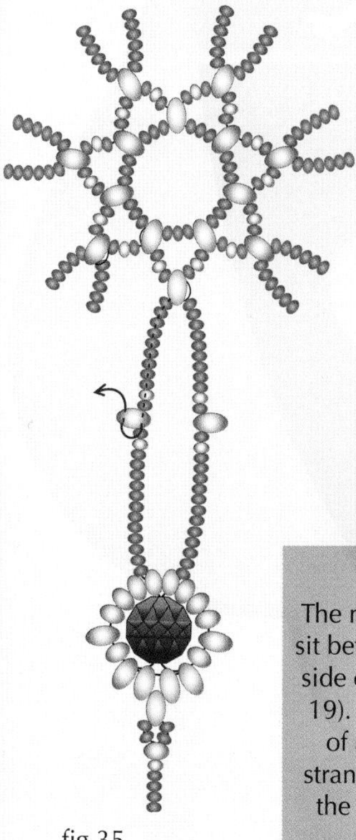

Extra Info....
The new cartouche motifs DO NOT sit between the two B beads at either side of a long loop (as made in Step 19). They link between one strand of a long loop and the adjacent strand of the next long loop around the bauble - make sure your link matches fig 36.

fig 35

21

Thread on 1D, 1B and 1D.

Pass the needle down through the outer hole of the adjacent B bead on the previous strand (fig 36).

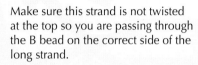

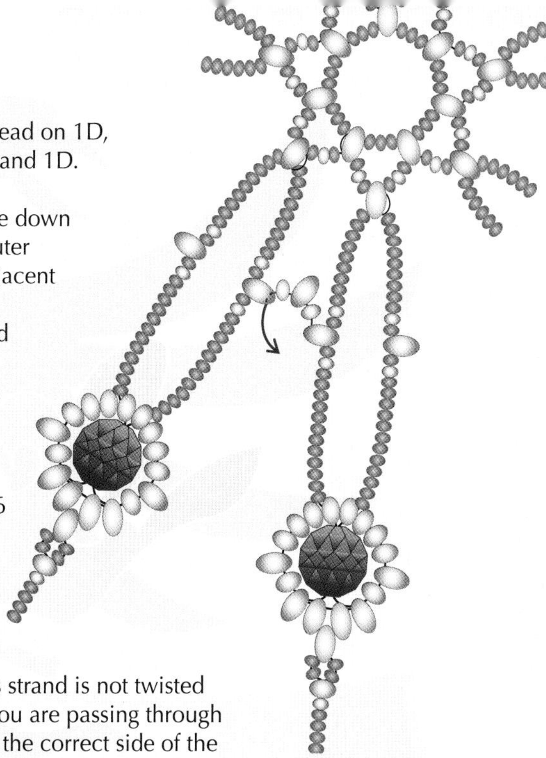

fig 36

Make sure this strand is not twisted at the top so you are passing through the B bead on the correct side of the long strand.

Thread on 1D, 1B, 1D, 1B, 1D, 1B and 1D. Pass up through the first B bead to complete the ring (fig 37).

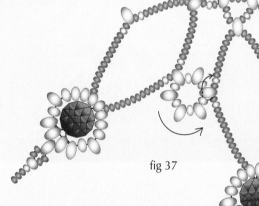

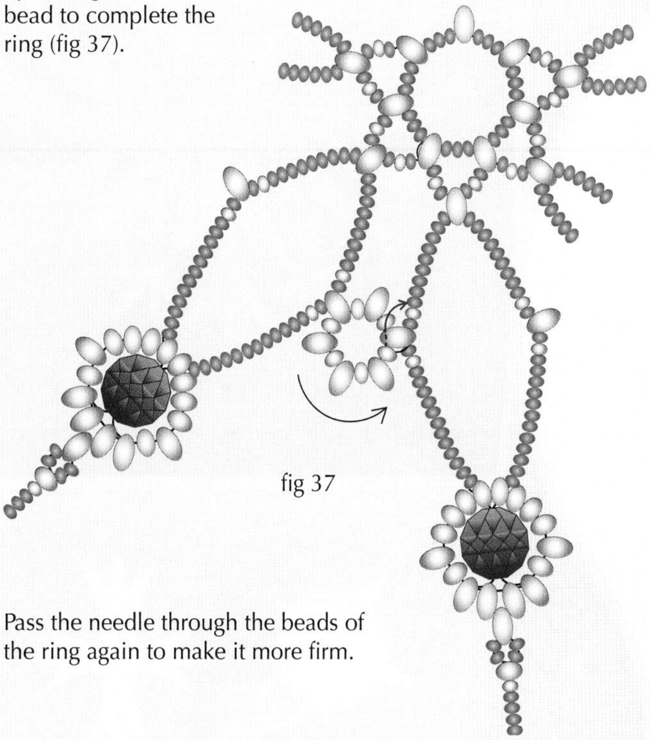

fig 37

Pass the needle through the beads of the ring again to make it more firm.

22 Pass through the following 1D and 1B to emerge from the B bead at the top of the ring.

Thread on 1E.

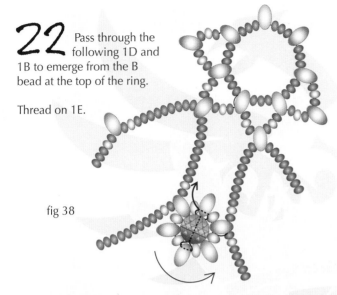

fig 38

Referring to fig 38 pass through the inner hole of the third B bead around the ring, back through the E bead and the B bead at the top of the ring to pull the E bead into the middle of the ring.

> ### Extra Info....
> As before, the E bead may sit a little proud of the frame rather than within the central space - this is fine as it makes for a bolder motif when it sits against the bauble. However, you must make sure that all the E beads of the cartouches sit on the outer faces of the motifs.

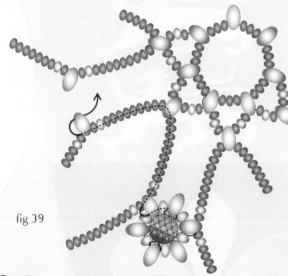

fig 39

23 Referring to fig 39 pass the needle through the following 1D and 1B of the ring.

Pass the needle up through the other hole on this B bead and the following 1A, 1C and 9A of the previous long strand, the B bead at the top and down the following 9A, 1C, 1A and 1B.

Pass up through the other hole of this B bead to be in the correct position to start the next E bead cartouche (fig 39).

Repeat from Step 21 six more times to create seven motifs in total. Finish with the needle emerging from the B bead at the top of the first long strand.

Finish off the thread ends from Steps 17 to 23 neatly and securely.

24 The Swags - There are long thread ends attached to each of the G bead cartouches. Choose the longest thread end and attach the needle.

This thread end will start the swags - you may need to swap to another of the loose thread ends to complete all seven swags.

Pass the needle through the beads of the cartouche frame to point upwards from the inner hole of the single B bead on one side of the frame. Pass down through the outer hole of this bead (fig 40).

fig 40

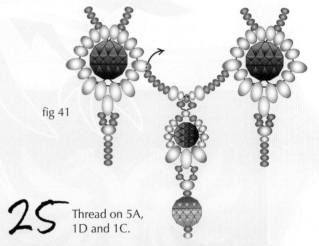

fig 41

25 Thread on 5A, 1D and 1C.

Pick up the first short strand made in Steps 10 to 16. Locate the 3A picot point at the H bead end of the strand. Pass the needle through the middle A bead of the picot and thread on 1C, 1D and 5A.

Pass the needle up through the outer hole of the corresponding B bead on the next G bead cartouche around (fig 41).

Referring to fig 42 reposition the needle through the lower beads of this cartouche to emerge ready to make the next swag.

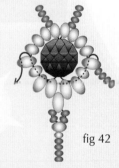

Repeat Step 25 until all seven swags are complete. Finish off all the remaining thread ends neatly and securely.

fig 42

Place the beading over the bauble.

26

The Crown - Prepare the needle with 1.2m of single thread and tie a keeper bead 15cm from the end.

Thread on twelve repeats of 1B and 1D. Pass the needle through the first B bead to bring the beads into a ring (as fig 29). Pass the needle through all the beads twice more to make the ring firm.

Pass the needle through the outer hole of the first B bead (fig 43).

Thread on 1B and pass through the outer hole of the next B bead around the ring (fig 44).

fig 43

Repeat to add 1B in each gap.

Pull the thread firmly to bring the beads up into a straight-sided drum.

Pass the needle through the row again to make the drum stable.

Pass the needle through the outer hole of the current B bead.

fig 44

27

Thread on 1B and pass through the outer hole of the next B around the drum (fig 45) - the new bead will form the first point of the crown.

Pass the needle through the inner hole of this B and the following 6B bead holes. Pass through the outer hole of the sixth B bead (fig 46).

The following figs show a side view of the work.

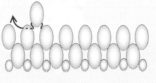

fig 45

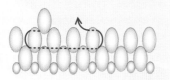

fig 46

28

Repeat Step 27 (fig 47).

Repeat Step 27 four more times to add six points in total. The needle should finish as in fig 46 (emerging just before the first B bead added in Step 27).

Pass through the following two B bead holes ready to add the A bead edging to the crown points (fig 48).

fig 47

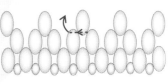

fig 48

29

Thread on 2A.

Referring to fig 49 pass the needle through the outer hole of the B bead at the top of the point and thread on 2A.

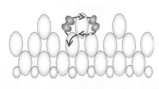

fig 49

Pass the needle through the corresponding B bead hole on the other side of the point and the following inner hole of the point bead (fig 49).

Pass the needle through the outer hole of the B point bead and thread on 2A, 1C and 1A.

Pass the needle back down the C bead to make a pointed tip (fig 50).

fig 50

Thread on 2A. Pass the needle through the outer hole of the B bead point (fig 51).

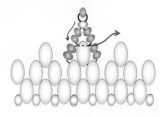

fig 51

30

Pass through the lower hole of this B bead and the following B bead hole to emerge at the start of the A bead edging.

Pass the needle up through the following 4A, the C and A of the tip.

Pass back down the 1C and 4A on the other side of the point.

Pass through the three B bead holes across the base of the embellishment to finish the edging on the first point (fig 52).

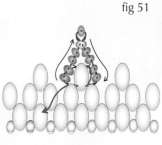

fig 52

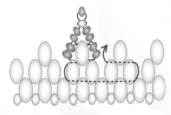

fig 53

fig 54

31 Reposition the needle to emerge in the correct place to start the next A bead edging (fig 53).

Repeat Steps 29 and 30.

The needle should be emerging at the start of the new A bead edging.

Pass the needle up through the first A bead only.

Pass down the last A bead of the previous point and up the first A of the new point (fig 54) - this extra stitch stabilises the points.

Complete the point as before and move onto the next point as in fig 53.

Repeat to add an A bead edging to all four remaining points making the link as in fig 54 between each pair of points. Don't forget to link the last A of the last point to the first A of the first point.

Pass the needle down to the bottom edge of the crown.

32 Place the crown over the top of the bauble so the bottom row corresponds to the foundation row made in Step 17. Use the attached thread to make five or six small stitches to secure the base row of the crown to the foundation row. Finish off all remaining thread ends neatly and securely.

33 The Hanging Loop - Prepare the needle with 1.2m of single thread and tie a keeper bead 15cm from the end.

Thread on 1D and 1K.

Pass the needle through the loop at the top of the bauble and back up through the K and D beads (fig 55).

Thread on 1A, 1C, 50A, 1C and 1A. Pass the needle down the D and K beads to draw up the loop.

Pass the needle through the bauble loop and back up the K and D beads.

fig 55

Pass the needle through the bead loop and the D and K connection to the bauble loop, at least three times, to strengthen, before finishing off the thread ends neatly and securely.

The fire polish faceted centre cartouches can be extended, linked and dangled to make a myriad of opulent designs. Make several individual cartouche motifs so they can be can arranged, and re-arranged, until you have a pleasing combination.

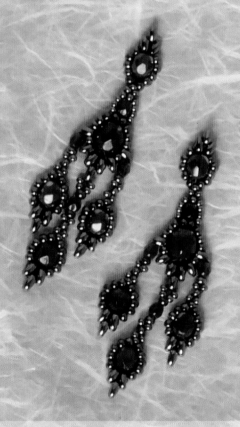

Baroque Earrings & Pendant

Just divine...deep red and gunmetal lustre earrings to bring 18th century elegance to a 21st century outfit. Centred on an 8mm fire polished faceted bead, each earring has three 6mm facet-centred cartouche dangles connected with 4mm faceted bead links. The earstud pads are glued to the back of the 6mm faceted beads at the top of the design for seamless style.

An elegant pendant necklace completes the set.

Etoile de Pearl

Swapping the fire polished facets for a more simple pearly round emphasises the Art Deco outline of the cartouche.

Bring six pearl-centred cartouches into a circle and you make a delightful star. Add a loop to make a festive decoration or stitch it directly onto a garment for a stunning motif.

Christmas Earrings

Four designs of jolly, festive earrings to brighten your day. Cute red-nosed reindeer to pull an important sleigh; quick and easy fir trees; elegant presents tied with a bow to leave below the tree; and stockings to hang up by the chimney: just waiting for that fellow in red to 'come-a-calling'.

Reindeer Earrings

Charming little characters to wear when delivering gifts to friends and family
– jingling bells are optional.

You Will Need

Materials

2g of size 15/0 frost transparent brown seed beads A
0.2g of size 15/0 lustred transparent grey seed beads B
0.2g of DB0697 semi-matt silver lined grey Delica beads C
Six size 6/0 black seed beads D
Two size 8/0 red chalk red seed beads E
Two 8mm topaz fire polished faceted beads H
Two 4mm gold plated jump rings
A pair of gold plated earfittings
Black size D beading thread

Tools

A size 13 beading needle
A pair of scissors to trim the threads

The Earrings are Made in Three Stages
The basic head shape is assembled and covered with brown beads.

The eyes, ears, antlers and nose are added.

The earfitting is attached with a jump ring.

1 The Head - Prepare the needle with 1.3m of single thread and tie a keeper bead 15cm from the end.

Thread on 1H and 1D - these two beads will form the core of the head and be referred to as 'the core'.

2 Thread on 15A. Pass through the core to make a strap of seed beads on one side (fig 1).

Make sure the two core beads are straight with the 15A forming a curve around them.

fig 1

Repeat Step 2 six more times to make seven straps in total. Make sure the straps do not cross over at either end of the core.

3 Thread on 3A, 8B and 4A. Pass down through the core to make an eighth strap.

Pass up through the first 3A and 2B of this strap and thread on 5A and 2B.

Pass up through the top 3A of the same strap (fig 2).
Pass down through the core.

The new seven-bead strap should pull in alongside the centre of the longer strap to 'fill-out' the width of the head profile a little. This double strap will form the centre front of the face.

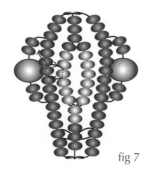

fig 2

4 Locate the 15A strap on the opposite side of the core to the double strap created in Step 3.

Pass up through the first 4A of this 15A and thread on 8A. Pass through the top 3A of the strap (fig 3).

Pass down through the core to complete a double strap in A beads.

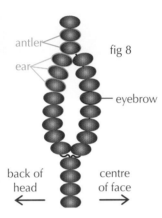

fig 3

5 There are three plain 15A straps, on each side, between the modified straps of Step 3 and Step 4.

Add an 8A short strap as in Step 4, to the middle plain 15A strap on each side of the core.

The core should now be covered in alternating single and double straps. The needle should be emerging from the bottom of the core.

6 The Eyes - Pass the needle up the first 3A at the bottom of the plain strap to one side of the centre front double strap.

Pass down the second A bead of the centre strap and back up the third A bead of the plain strap to make a Square stitch (fig 4). Pass up through the following 3A.

Thread on 2A, 1D and 2A.

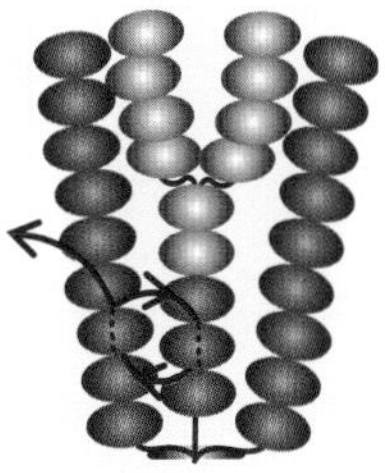

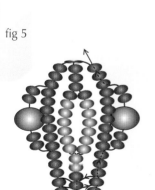

fig 4

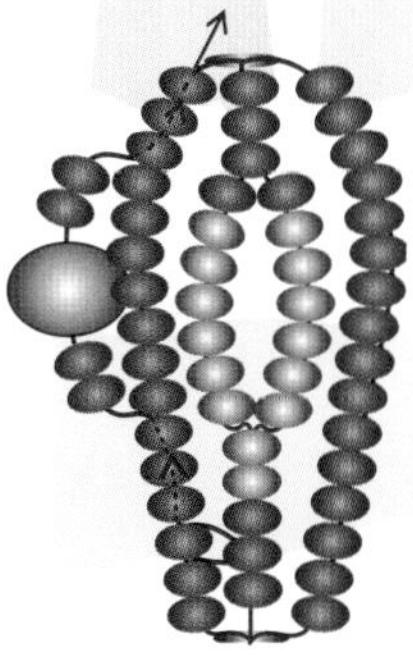

fig 5

Pass up through the top 3A of the same plain strap pushing the new short strap to the outer edge of the plain strap (fig 5).
Pass down through the core.

Repeat Step 6 on the other side of the centre front (fig 6).

fig 6

7 Pass the needle up the bottom 10A of the first strap of Step 6 to emerge alongside the centre front strap.

Count nine beads up from the bottom of the adjacent centre front row and pass down through this bead.

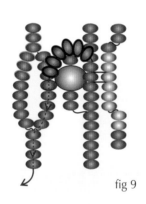

fig 7

Pass up through the tenth A bead of the original row to make a Square stitch (fig 7). Pass up through the following 1A.

Alongside the eye bead row is a double strap of A beads. This double strap supports the antlers, the eyebrow and the ears.

Referring to fig 8 you can see the antlers attach to beads 2 and 3 of the top single section.

The eyebrow connects to the 8A section closest to the eye.

The ear is supported by the top three beads of the other 8A section so that it sits a little further back around the head (fig 8).

antler

ear

fig 8

eyebrow

back of head

centre of face

←   →

8 Thread on 6A for the eyebrow and arch the beads over the eye. Referring to fig 8 count 4A down the adjacent 8A section of the double row to locate the bead indicated for the eyebrow.

Referring to fig 9 pass down through this bead and the following 8A to emerge at the bottom of the row.

fig 9

Do not pass through the core. Referring to fig 10, which shows the repositioning of the needle across the base of the core, repeat from Step 7 on the other side of the centre front row to make the second eyebrow.

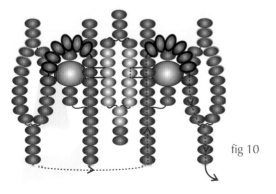

fig 10

When the second eyebrow is complete pass through the core to the top of the head.

9 The Ears - Referring to fig 8 pass down through the top 5A beads of the double strap to emerge from the middle A bead of the 3A indicated for the ear.

Thread on 2B and 5A.

Pass the needle back down the fourth A bead and thread on 1A. Pass the needle down the 2A above the 2B and the 2B to pull the new A bead parallel to the third A. Pass through the A bead on the strap in the same direction (fig 11).

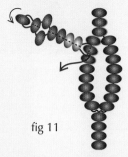

fig 11

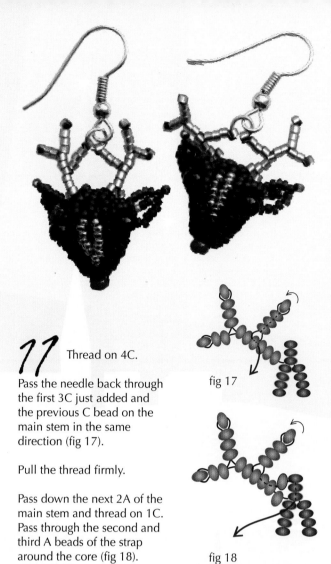

Pass through the next 1A along and thread on 6A.

Pass the needle up through the first of the two parallel A beads and the following 2A (fig 12).

fig 12

Pass down through the previous 1A and the other parallel A bead. Thread on 4A.
Pass through the top 3A beads on the 8A section of the double strap (fig 13).

Pass down through the remaining beads of the strap and up through the core.

Repeat Step 9 on the other side of the head to add the second ear.

fig 13

10 The Antlers - Referring to fig 8 the antlers attach to the second and third A beads at the top of the strap.

Pass the needle down through the top 3A of the strap and thread on 10C. Leaving aside the last 1C pass back through the preceding 3C to make a 4C branch (fig 14).

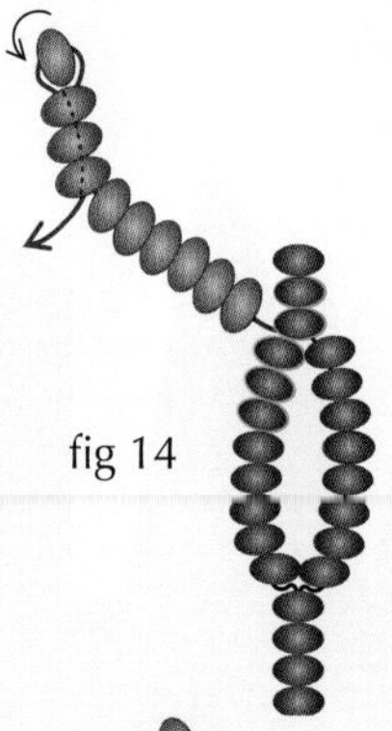

fig 14

Thread on 3C. Leaving aside the last 1C pass the needle back through the preceding 2C (fig 15).

These two branches have to be reinforced.

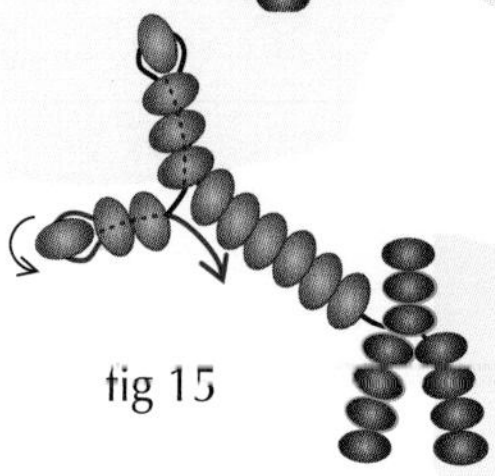

fig 15

Referring to fig 16 pass up and down the 4C branch and up and down the 3C branch. Pass down the following 3C of the main stem (fig 16).

Pull the thread firmly so the two branches stand proud.

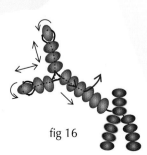

fig 16

11 Thread on 4C.

Pass the needle back through the first 3C just added and the previous C bead on the main stem in the same direction (fig 17).

fig 17

Pull the thread firmly.

Pass down the next 2A of the main stem and thread on 1C. Pass through the second and third A beads of the strap around the core (fig 18).

fig 18

Pass the needle back up to the first 6C of the stem and strengthen the top two branches of the antlers again (as fig 16) passing back down to the base of the stem without strengthening the side branch added in fig 18.

Pass down the double strap to the bottom of the core.

12 Thread on 1E for the nose and pass through the core. Try to position the nose bead horizontally across the base of the head with the hole running in line with the core hole - its position will be reinforced when you finish the second antler.

Repeat Steps 10 and 11 to add the second antler on the other side of the head.

Pass through the E bead nose and straight up through the core - this should secure the nose flat against the base of the core. Remove the keeper bead and finish off both thread ends neatly and securely.

13 Complete the Earring - Twist open a jump ring. Carefully thread the ring through the C beads at the tips of the lowest two antler branches - the rings will fit with a gentle wiggle. Close the jump ring and add the earfitting.

Repeat to make the second earring.

Christmas Present Earrings

Beautifully wrapped with a perfect bow – does your parcel contain expensive scent, hand–knitted socks or a wonderful selection of beads ?

The Earrings are Made in Four Stages
The present box is made in Square stitch first.

The band to wrap around the box is made next.

The bow is made at the end of the band.

The band is wrapped around the box and the earfitting is added to the centre of the bow.

You Will Need

Materials

2.8g of DB0610 silver lined dark violet Delica beads A
1.5g of size 15/0 semi-matt silver lined red seed beads B
Two size 8/0 silver lined red seed beads C
Two 4mm soldered jump rings
Two 4mm standard jump rings
A pair of gold plated earfittings
Red size D beading thread

Tools

A size 13 beading needle
A pair of scissors to trim the threads

---

1 The Present Box - Prepare the needle with 1.3m of single thread and tie a keeper bead 15cm from the end.

Thread on 10A for the first row.

Thread on 1A to start the new row. Pass back through the last bead of the previous row and through the new A bead again, bringing the holes in the two beads parallel to make a Square stitch (fig 1).

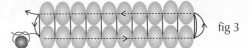

fig 1

fig 2

2 Thread on 1A and make a Square stitch to attach this new A to the next bead along the previous row (fig 2). Repeat to the end of the row.

To bring the beads neatly into line pass the needle through the 10A beads of the first row and the 10A just added (fig 3). You need to make this neatening pass each time you complete a row.

fig 3

3 Work twelve more rows of 10A.

Join the first row to the last row with a Square-stitched seam (fig 4).

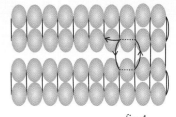

fig 4

4 The Band Around the Box - The ribbon that stretches around the box attaches to the middle 2A of the last row.

Pass the needle through the first 6A of the last row.

fig 5

Thread on 2B. Square stitch this 2B to the last 2A passed through (fig 5).

Neaten the row as before passing through the same 2A of the box and the 2B of the band.

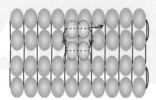

fig 6

Thread on 2B and Square stitch to the previous 2B (fig 6).

Neaten as before with a second pass of the needle.

Repeat nineteen times to make a 2B band, 21 rows long.

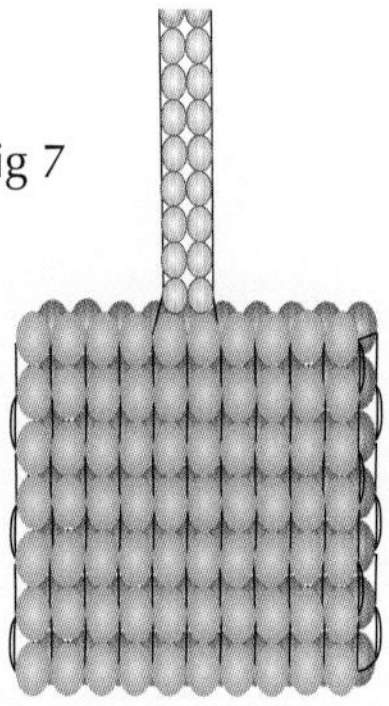

fig 7

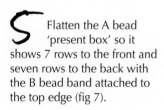

5 Flatten the A bead 'present box' so it shows 7 rows to the front and seven rows to the back with the B bead band attached to the top edge (fig 7).

Wrap the band around the box.

Do the first and last rows of 2B meet, or is there a gap? If there is a gap, work one more row of 2B.

To make the work easier to hold, the bow is made at the end of the 2B band before it is secured around the box.

6 The Bow - The bow is also made in Square stitch.

It is important that you DO NOT make the neatening pass of the needle after each row or the beads will become congested with thread. Instead the needle weaves back though the rows when each element is completed (see figs 15, 16 and 21).

Thread on 1C.

Pass through the last 2B of the band and back through the C bead (fig 8).

This C bead is the centre of the bow and supports both bow loops.

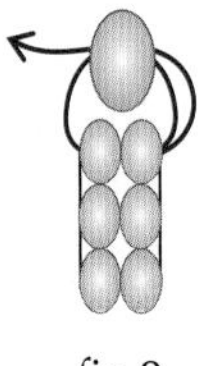

fig 8

7 Thread on 2B and pass back through the C bead (fig 9).

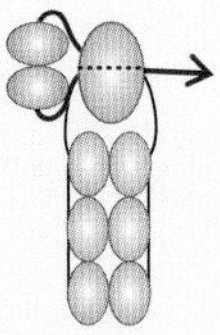

Thread on 2B and pass back through the C bead.
Pass through the new 2B on this side of the C bead to point towards the band (fig 10).

This 2B is Row One of the bow loop.

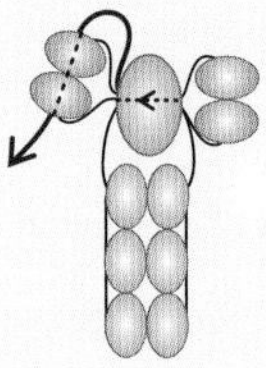

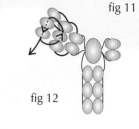

fig 9

fig 10

8 Row Two - Thread on 3B and using a single Square stitch attach to the 2B of Row One (fig 11).

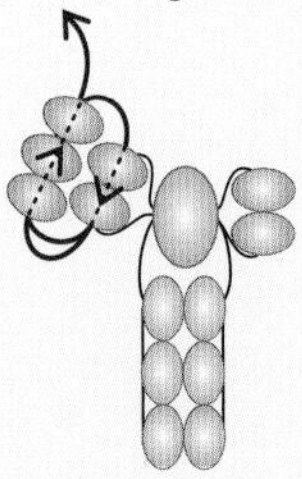

Row Three - Thread on 1B and Square stitch to the last 1B of the previous row.

Square stitch 2B to the next 1B bead along (fig 12) and 1B to the first B bead of the previous row (4B in total).

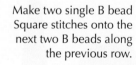

fig 11

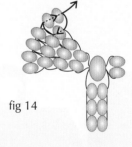

fig 12

fig 13

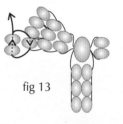

Row Four - Thread on 2B and Square stitch onto the last B of the previous row (fig 13).

Make two single B bead Square stitches onto the next two B beads along the previous row.

Finish with a 2B stitch onto the first 1B of the previous row (6B in total) (fig 14).

fig 14

Referring to fig 15 pass the needle back through the Square stitch rows just worked. Thread on 1B and pass back through the C bead (fig 15).

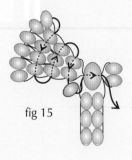

fig 15

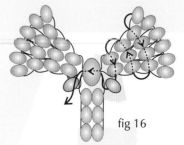

fig 16

9 Pass through the 2B on this side of the C to point towards the band (as fig 10).

Repeat Step 8 on this side of the C bead to complete the second bow loop (fig 16).

10

The needle should be emerging from the C bead (as fig 16).

Pass through the single B bead added in fig 15 to point towards the band (fig 17).

This B bead is Row One of the bow tail on this side of the C bead.

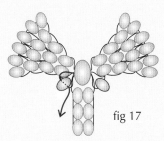

fig 17

Referring to fig 18 -
Row Two - Square stitch 2B onto the 1B bead.

Row Three - Add 2B to the previous row of 2B with a single Square stitch.

Row Four - Add 3B to the previous row of 2B with a single Square stitch (fig 18).

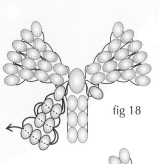

fig 18

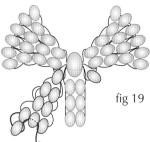

fig 19

11

Row Five -
Thread on 1B.

Pass the needle forward through the middle B of the previous row (fig 19).

Thread on 1B. Pass the needle back through the 3B of Row Four (fig 20).

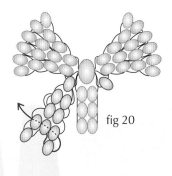

fig 20

Pass back through the beads of Row Three, Row Two and the single B bead of Row One. Pass through the C bead (fig 21).

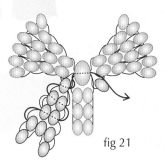

fig 21

Repeat Steps 10 and 11 on this side of the C bead to complete the bow.

Finish with the needle emerging from the C bead as in fig 21.

12

Complete the Earring - Stitch a soldered jump ring to the C bead with at least three passes of thread.

Wrap the band around the present box so the C bead at the centre of the bow sits at the top of the box with the bow tails pointing downwards. Square stitch the last row of the band to the first row of the band.

Stitch the first row of the band to the C bead.

Pass the needle into the A beads along the top edge of the present box.

13

Use a single Square stitch to secure the lower tip of the bow loop to the end of the top row of the box (see fig 22).

Pass the needle down through the edge beads of the box and secure the tip of the bow tail to the edge of the box where they touch (fig 22).

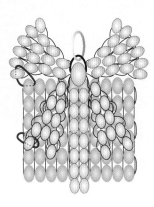

fig 22

Repeat on the other edge of the box.

Finish off the thread ends neatly and securely.

Add the earfitting to the soldered jump ring at the top with a standard (opening) jump ring and repeat to make the second earring.

Christmas Stocking Earrings

✦ ✦ ✦

Get ready for Santa with these adorable little stockings. Made in Herringbone stitch they look as though they were knitted by the fairy on the Christmas tree.

You Will Need

Materials

2.0g of size 15/0 semi-matt silver lined red seed beads A
0.6g of size 15/0 frost chalk white seed beads B
0.2g of size 15/0 silver lined green seed beads C
Two size 8/0 chalk red seed beads D
Two 4mm gold plated jump rings
A pair of gold plated earfittings
Red size D beading thread

Tools

A size 13 beading needle
A pair of scissors to trim the threads

The Earrings are Made in Four Stages

The band at the top of the stocking is made in Ladder stitch.

The main sock is worked in Herringbone stitch.

A contrast colour heel is added to the sock.

The holly sprig and top loop are added.

1 The Top Band - Prepare the needle with 1.3m of single thread and tie a keeper bead 15cm from the end.

Thread on 8B.
Pass the needle back up the first 4B and down the second 4B to make two columns (fig 1).

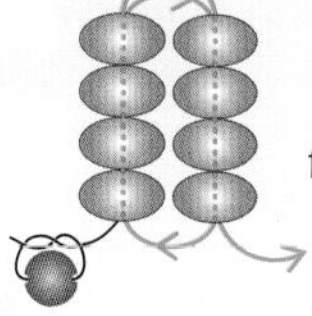

fig 1

Thread on 4B.
Pass down the previous column and up through the new beads (fig 2).

Thread on 4B and pass up the previous 4B and down the new 4B (fig 3).

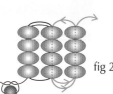
fig 2

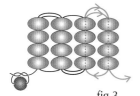
fig 3

This is Ladder stitch.

Add eight more stitches of 4B to make a row of twelve columns in total.

2 Pass the needle up through the first column, down the last column and up the first column to bring the row into a drum-shaped ring (fig 4).

fig 4

3 The Main Sock - This is made in Herringbone stitch. The beads are added in pairs. The columns take on a chevron appearance which resembles a knitted sock very well.

Extra Info....
Figs 5 to 25 show the sock upside-down as that is the easiest way to hold the work while you are stitching the Herringbone section.

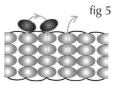
fig 5

Row 1 - Thread on 2A. Pass the needle down the top 2B of the next column and up the top 2B of the following column (fig 5).

Thread on 2A and repeat the previous stitch (fig 6).

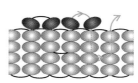
fig 6

Repeat four more times to complete the row.

4 Pass the needle up through the first A bead of the row just completed to be in the correct position to start the next row (fig 7).

Row 2 - Thread on 2A.

Pass down the following A bead of the previous row and up through the next A along (fig 8).

Repeat five times.

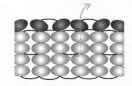

fig 7

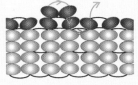

fig 8

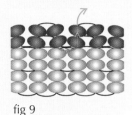

fig 9

As before, complete the row by passing up through the first bead of the row ready to start the next (fig 9).

You should be able to see the start of the chevron effect.

Repeat Row 2 four more times to make six rows in total. The work now splits to leave a gap for the heel to be added in Steps 13 and 14.

5 Thread on 2A.

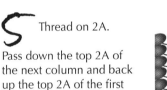

fig 10

Pass down the top 2A of the next column and back up the top 2A of the first column.
Pass up through the first 1A of the 2A just added (fig 10).

Repeat this stitch twice more to make a column 2A wide and 3A high (fig 11).

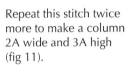

fig 11

This column forms the 'front of the sock'.

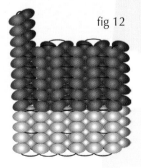

fig 12

Flatten the drum section of the sock so this column runs along the fold (fig 12).

6 Thread on 2A and Ladder stitch to the previous 2A (fig 13).

Repeat to add a second stitch of 2A to the first (fig 14).

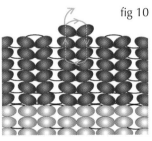

fig 13

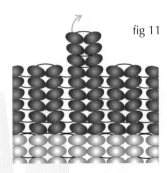

fig 14

7 Add eight more 2A Ladder stitches to make a band of 10 columns of 2A.

Referring to fig 15 bend the band around to make a drum and stitch the last 2A added to the other side of the 'front of the sock' column.

Note - the new drum is placed above the previous rows, not to the other side of the 'front of the sock' column (fig 15).

fig 15

8 For clarity figs 16-20 show the top rows of the work stretched out flat although you will be working in the round as before.

You need to add two more rows of Herringbone stitch.

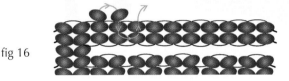

fig 16

Referring to fig 16 thread on 2A, pass down the top 1A of the previous column of 2A and up the next to start the new row of Herringbone stitch (fig 16).

Repeat to the end of the row.

Reposition the needle to start a new row as before, and repeat to add one more row of Herringbone stitch.

9 Closing the Toe of the Sock - Make the first stitch of the next row as before with 2A and reposition the needle for the next stitch.

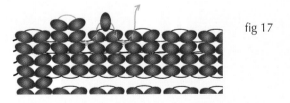

fig 17

Make this stitch with 1A only (fig 17).

Alternate the next four stitches with 2A, 1A, 2A, and 1A (the last 1A stitch is across the 'front of the sock' column).

fig 18

Reposition the needle as before for the next row (fig 18).

13
Reposition the needle to emerge from the heel gap end of the A bead column adjacent to the 'front of the sock' column (fig 22).

fig 22

fig 23

10
Thread on 1A.

Pass down the next A bead around, through the single A at the top of the next column and up through the first A of the following column (fig 19).

fig 19

Repeat twice finishing with the needle passing through the last single A of the previous row ('front of the sock' column).

11
The A bead at the top of the 'front of the sock' column and the three single A beads from the previous row are now linked to complete the toe.

Referring to fig 20 throughout pass through the next 1A and thread on 3A.
Pass through the following 1A from the previous row.
Thread on 3A and pass through the next 1A from the previous row.
Pass through the 1A on the 'front of the sock' column to complete the row (fig 20).

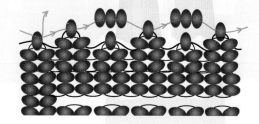

fig 20

12
If necessary reinstate the fold (from fig 12) so the two blocks of 3A beads just added sit parallel to one another.

Pass the needle through to the first of these 3A sections and stitch this 3A to the parallel 3A to seal the toe of the sock (fig 21).

fig 21   end view

14
The Heel - The heel is made with a series of stitches across the gap. The stitches increase in length to create a V of beads.

Thread on 2A. Pass through the corresponding A bead on the other side of the heel gap and back up the next A bead along (fig 23).

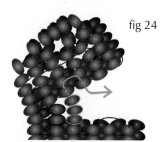

fig 24

Thread on 3A.

Pass through the corresponding A bead on the other side of the heel gap and back down the next A bead along (fig 24).

fig 25

Make the third stitch with 2A, 1B and 2A.

Make the fourth stitch with 2A, 2B and 2A.

Make the fifth stitch with 2A, 3B and 2A (fig 25).

Reverse the sequence as you work across the other side of the sock to complete the triangle on each face.

Following fig 26 make a series of small Square stitches to link the rows of the heel together.

Make an extra Square stitch to link the two sections of 3A on the outer edge of the heel.

fig 26

Repeat fig 26 on the reverse of the sock.
These last few stitches bring the sock into a sealed tube.

Turn the sock so it is the right way up.

15

Adding the Holly and the Loop -
Pass the needle up through the sock
to emerge two B beads down from the top edge
of the sock and two rows from the heel edge.
This is where you add the holly sprig.

Thread on 3C.
Pass the needle back
down the second C bead
(fig 27).

fig 27

Thread on 3C and pass the
needle back down the second C
just added (fig 28).

fig 28

Repeat this stitch
three more times.

Pass though the first
C bead of the sprig in
the same direction to
bring the C beads into
a spiky ring (fig 29).

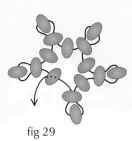

fig 29

Attach the spiky ring onto the B beads of the top
band of the sock with a small stitch leaving a
gap in the centre of the ring for the D bead.

Using a small stitch, add 1D in the centre of the
ring.

16

Pass the needle up through the B
beads of the band to emerge on the
top edge of the band at the heel edge of the
sock.

Thread on 5A.
Pass down the adjacent
column of the heel edge to
make a loop (fig 30).

Reinforce the loop with two
more passes of thread and
finish off both thread ends
neatly and securely.

fig 30

Add the earfitting with a jump ring.

Repeat to make the
second earring adding
the holly to the opposite
face of the sock to create
a matching pair.

If you want a fat sock
(so it appears to be full
of presents) use a tiny
piece of polythene to
stuff the cavity.

Fir Tree Earrings

Cute, festive and very quick to make.

You Will Need

Forty-two scarab green or
bottle green Twin beads A

Four frost brown AB size 6/0
seed beads B

Six size 6/0 seed beads to
match the Twin beads C

Four size 8/0 seed beads to
match the Twin beads D

Two headpins
A pair of earfittings
Green size D beading thread

Each earring is made from a stack of Twin bead rings.

Prepare the needle with 1m of double
thread. Thread on 9A. Pass the needle
through the same hole on the first A
bead to make a ring (fig 1).

fig 1

Pass the needle through the following eight beads
to make the ring firm and so the needle thread emerges alongside
the tail threads. Pull both sides of the thread very firmly to make the
ring as tight as you can.

Tie the thread ends together with an
overhand knot (fig 2).

Repeat to make two more knots pulling
them down tightly into the same gap
between the beads.

fig 2

Dab the knots with a little clear nail polish or glue. Cut off the
needle thread 1cm from the knot and leave the ring to dry.

Repeat to make a ring with 7A beads.
Repeat to make a ring with 5A beads.

When the knots are dry trim off the
thread ends neatly.

Thread 2B onto a headpin.
Thread on the 9A ring.
Thread on 1D and push it into the centre
of the 9A ring.
Thread on 1C, the 7A ring, 1C, the 5A ring, 1C and 1D (fig 3).

fig 3

Trim the headpin to 8mm above the top bead and turn a loop using
round-nosed pliers. Add the earfitting and repeat to make the
second earring.

Index & Suppliers

All of the materials used in this book should be available in any good bead shop or online. If you are new to beading, or need more supplies, the companies listed below run fast, efficient mail order services, hold large stocks of all of the materials you will need in their stores and give good, well-informed, friendly advice on all aspects of beading and beading needs.

In the UK

Spellbound Bead Co
47 Tamworth Street
Lichfield
Staffordshire
WS13 6JW
01543 417650

www.spellboundbead.co.uk

Spellbound Bead Co supplied all of the materials for the samples shown.

You can buy the beads for these projects loose (wholesale and retail), in counted bead packs or as fully illustrated kits.

In USA

Fire Mountain Gems
One Fire Mountain Way
Grants Pass
OR 97526 - 2373
Tel: + 800 355 2137
www.firemountaingems.com

Shipwreck Beads
8560 Commerce Place Dr.NE
Lacey
WA 98516
Tel: + 800 950 4232
www.shipwreckbeads.com